Discovering the Realm Beyond Appearance

Like the river on entering the ocean loses its identity, so the individual upon entering the stream of consciousness loses his own sparate existence. Let us talk over how this works in practice.

Consciousness uses the brain, expresses itself through it, but consciousness is not in the brain, the brain is in consciousness.

Inquire directly into consciousness, your real nature. The best way for you to pursue this pathless path is not through research into science, which, as you rightly state, is thoroughly dualistic, but through your own meditation, your own inquiry, so that you may get the necessary insights first-hand and not from hearsay, and eventually a taste of the non-dual, the timeless, which alone is real.

DISCOVERING THE REALM BEYOND APPEARANCE

Pointers to the Inexpressible

Robert Powell

New Age Books

ISBN: 81-7822-130-6

First Indian Edition: Delhi, 2005

(Published by arrangement with Blue Dove Press, California)

First Edition: USA, 1999

Published by
NEW AGE BOOKS
A-44 Naraina Phase-I
New Delhi-110 028 (INDIA)
Email: nab@vsnl.in
Website: www.newagebooksindia.com

For Sale in Southeast Asia Only

Printed in India
at Shri Jainendra Press
A-45 Naraina Phase-I, New Delhi-110 028

All living beings are sentient or conscious to a greater or lesser extent, but only human beings have the potential to be conscious of their consciousness — yet few are. To be conscious of the consciousness — herein lies man's potential for Greatness and his key to freedom.

— Robert Powell

CONTENTS

Although the material in this book is self-contained, these discussions are in many ways a continuation of the earlier work *Dialogues on Reality*, but in this volume the questions and answers have been grouped together according to subject matter rather than chronologically.

Discovering the Realm Beyond Appearance

1

Entering the Stream of Consciousness

Like the river on entering the ocean loses its identity, so the individual upon entering the stream of consciousness loses his own separate existence. Let us talk over how this works in practice.

Everyone refers intuitively to himself as a basic point of reference from which he observes the multifarious objects of this world, whereby he makes himself automatically the subject. There is an endless stream of consciousness or flow of thoughts and we think there is the thinker, who is the ultimate subject. However, if one inquires somewhat more deeply into this, as has been done, for example, so brilliantly by the late J. Krishnamurti, one discovers that there really is only thought and no separate thinker. The latter is a construct of and in thought, a picture or a concept with no substance of itself. However, when a lot of these pictures or thought structures are held together in time and so given a false sense of continuity by memory, this gives the pseudo entity some imaginary substance or reality. Then when this pseudo entity associates itself, or gets identified with an apparently real body, the deception is compounded. Because the body is so clearly mortal and vulnerable, the idea arises that the "I" is equally vulnerable and short-lived. But how does the situation appear when there is only thought and no thinker at all, when the thought is seen to be impersonal and belonging to neither you nor me? Is the thinker then not just another object? Then it is seen very clearly that the whole idea of our mortality and fear of death are based on a misunderstanding of the nature of that "I." If there is no thinker in the first place, there can be neither birth nor death. All the happenings to the body and the world are being witnessed continually. That is very clearly the case and something no one can dispute. The question, however, is by whom is the witnessing?

Whereas previously it was thought that events were witnessed intermittently, so long as the body-mind entity persisted, now it is clear that witnessing goes on forever and regardless of any circumstances. It is not even correct to state that this witnessing goes on by either you or me, or by someone else, because the latter entities are nonexistent and live only in our imagination in the form of evanescent thoughts. Witnessing can be seen to be taking place eternally by my Self, the real, impersonal "I" who stands beyond the stream of consciousness as the rearmost background upon which the entire phenomenal world is constantly being projected.

Another way to look at this problem is to see that the

"I" or the insight of "I am" at any one particular time is associated with a particular body — that is, our perspective is always from one particular body-mind entity. It does not occur to us to view the perspective from another body-mind entity as being equally that of our own. It is a circular situation: because we are identified solely with one particular body-mind entity, our perception is of seeing a world populated by similar body-mind entities, rather than seeing the real situation. The truth is that bodies by themselves are mere corpses, without sentience, in the absence of the Self that vitalizes them and that these bodies as multiple appearances are projected upon the unicity of the "I."

Thus, it is the bodies that come and go, but that which is associated with the body does not come and go. It is only when one has identified oneself with a particular body that this is difficult to understand. In other words, there has to be a seeing through or a "transcendence" of this erroneous idea before the truth can dawn upon one. When it does, there is this extraordinary realization of true selfhood, which brings with it an immense vitality and true liberation. Let us therefore concentrate our search on the feeling of "I-ness" when all our life we are constantly referring to this "I," without actually knowing It. The most direct way towards this end is realizing the "I-ness," on the deepest level, which remains after all the false "I" notions have been discarded, all the false thought structures that have given rise to imaginary self entities have been voided. With the dissipation of all identification with a body image, one has taken the final step into freedom and there is a realization that one's deepest "I," which is one's actual "I," has never not been in existence and also will never not be in existence. Everyone always refers to him-or herself with one simple word, "I,"and all these different "I"s refer to mySelf or the Self. Here I favor the term "I" over "mySelf" because the latter is begging the question as to its real nature. It tends to lead us astray, because the personal pronoun "my" already implies a particular identity or "person." Thus, once I am out of the habitual identification with body, I am no longer the end product of the identification but I recognize myself as That, which in its ignorant state ever tends to identify itself with a body, and therefore I am That before identification with body. My existence is forever: there is no interruption in my being, I am the Self always, whether awake or asleep, whether in or with this body or that body. I am ever only in the present, for I am Presence or Existence itself. It is the same "I" that from time immemorial has undergone endless experiences, or better, has endless experiences projected on It and will ever undergo fresh experiences. And because it incorporates the whole of time, it is in itself not touched by time at all. It is the same "I" that is to be associated with innumerable bodies and has the tendency to identify with any of these particular bodies, but also the freedom to refrain from such identification.

In sum, I am pure Awareness or Consciousness in which all entities, the whole world, make its appearance. Because that pure Consciousness is prior to everything, and therefore void of any attributes, in its own nature it is designed as pure Emptiness. But because nothing can exist outside that Emptiness, it can equally well be referred to as Fullness. On account of these paradoxes, it can perhaps be best referred to as the Unnamable.

Once one has got in touch with the deepest "I" that lies before any conceptual or mental structures have gotten a foothold, there is a direct experience — or perhaps a better word would be "realization" — of one's Immortality. Then there is no going back anymore towards Ignorance. Although outwardly one may appear no different than before, inwardly one can never be the same.

As an initial step to get perhaps some inkling of this utterly different vision, it might well be useful as an initial rough approximation to think of the unchanging "I" being sequentially associated with an endless series of different bodies in a long chain of incarnations. So I can see myself discarding and assuming body after body in an unending sequence. There is an unchanging succession of fresh waves on the ocean, but looking beneath surface appearance, there is only the everlasting ocean. Another symbolic categorization one finds in the sacred literature, where the "I" has been portrayed as a charioteer, manning the chariot of the body. The chariots may change but there is only one charioteer throughout who successively mans a multitude of chariots.

But in truth, all this imagery is only to prepare, to orient us, towards the ultimate explosive realization that only the "I" ever exists, one's true Selfhood. Neither the bodies nor the chariots are real! They are simply projections onto the Real or the eternal Self. These projections have been given some apparent reality by a faulty identification of Consciousness with these apparitions. The moment I see that I am not my body, nor body-mind, but nothing but pure Consciousness, the ultimate background to my perceiving world, and that this body or world can have no existence apart from me, I have broken the spell which kept me in ignorance.

Constantly thinking in a particular mode gives a certain reality to that thought, leads one to become that conceptualization. The body image as being primarily physical in nature fills the mind's need for concreteness and permanence. But even that sense of security vanishes upon inquiry into the nature of the physical world, with the resultant recognition that it is also only of the nature of consciousness. The body image is really underpinned by the separation between mind and matter as two utterly different realms — the "tangible" and the "intangible" — which most of us have uncritically accepted. It is this latter split which in my view lies at the bottom of all confusion about our fundamental self-nature. Then "when one comes to one's senses," in this important respect, in first instance one states "everything is 'mental'" — the first step into non-duality. But immediately such a pronouncement has been made, even that is seen to be false, because it can no longer convey any meaning. To define something as "mental" made sense only so long as there was the "physical." Thus, the moment it is seen that the physical does not really exist as such, the mental also disappears from view. What remains then is simply: "everything *is*." And that "everything," that Totality, can only be the Consciousness or the Self.

LIBERATION FROM THE CONTENTS

Now where does one go from here? Up to now one has simply laid the right foundation for the *advaitic* mode of life, which is life in tune with what *is* on every level of one's existence and functioning. One has fundamentally weakened an ingrained tendency to view everything through the eyes of body-identification, and so secondarily also, mind-identification. It is an essential first step, but traces of the *dvaitic* mode of life still remain, for the habits of one's egoic existence have not yet been fully rooted out. The question therefore is: How does one actually merge into the Consciousness without leaving a trace behind? If one has understood what one truly is, then what are left, what still manifests, are the *vasanas* — the energies and tendencies that continue from past incarnations. These *vasanas* that have the dynamics of an apparent ego have to be stirred up so that they may be dealt with and burned up.

Essential to transformation at this point is the interface of the timely and the timeless. Time means past and future, and thereby thought, concept. So long as thought, based on the concept of an "I" — that is, physical and mental separateness — continues, there is *samsara* or misery. So what is involved is a slowing down of the thought process based on experience. All experience being based on the past, the awareness is shifted away from contents.

Essential to the interface of happiness/unhappiness is Time. The present moment, this very moment, never disturbs us, since it falls just in between two thoughts. It is always the moment that is just past, or past for some time and remembered, that gives rise to the thought disturbing our peace; but the background is ever peaceful. And the future is the past continued.

The feeling of a wanting, of a lack, always arises from thought, which is spawned by the mind. To go beyond the mind is to step out of time and become purely and totally this moment, pure Presence. In this Presence, nothing else exists. It is pure Nothingness — the timeless or Eternal because it lies beyond change. Change is part of the contents of consciousness — Consciousness itself being the changeless background upon which the mind projects its shadow play of *samskara*. Thus, "this moment" is "thisness," pure Existence, which is synonymous with pure Consciousness and Bliss — *satchitananda*.

Most of us believe that meditation is the required avenue towards enlightenment. But meditation, at best, can only be an incipient approach, because it is still a movement within the ordinary consciousness, within the mind, and therefore a modification of the contents of consciousness. What we are pointing to is a going beyond the mind, a liberation from the contents of the mind. The mind must go out of business; that is, out of any business that is not properly its business. That is why the late Indian sage Sri Poonja emphasized that the main requirement is just to keep quiet, and see what happens. That is, the mind is to "just say no" to anything that is not properly within its domain of activity. When we go to sleep at night, are we bothered by all the encumbrances of the waking state? No, we have put all that aside and enjoy our being in freedom, enjoying fully the bliss of deep sleep. Upon waking, we again assume all the burdens that arise from the flow of time, that are associated with the past. Poonjaji calls the past a "graveyard" and admonishes us to leave it severely alone. Thought is ever this past, and Ramana Maharshi advises the tracing of every thought back to its source in the Heart. If one does that, one finds that thoughts always depend on a conceptual "I" and that, in the absence of the latter, no thought arises. Tracing any thought to its source exposes the conceptual and unreal "I."

What is consciousness?

That this question is raised at all shows the extent of alienation from our real self. The consciousness is the closest thing to us, because it is what we are as manifestation. When you look at an object, what you observe is still consciousness, since all objects appear in consciousness. Just think for a moment of a movie projected onto the screen. All the persons and objects in the movie appear on the screen; we normally forget about the screen because we are so fascinated by the play of light and dark on that screen. It is just like that with Consciousness; it is the screen upon which the world is projected.

Consciousness is the only thing that we can lay claim to. And since it also is the only thing that exists and all other things find their origin in it, consciousness cannot be defined in terms of these other things; however, the other things can and must ultimately be defined in terms of consciousness. But as in the story of the tenth man, it is seldom taken into consideration when taking stock of our apparent being in this world.

Consciousness is the totality of our experience, but we have lost view of that because of a concentration on particular objects within the field of awareness. And our alienation has resulted from identification with the body-mind complex. Dispel that identification and you will realize Consciousness.

If we are Consciousness, how is it that we can, as we say, "lose consciousness" or become unconscious?

It may only appear that way because we are not perceptive enough. It may be that through our present way of life, our sensate lifestyle, perception of our existence has been dulled to such an extent that we are unable to realize our ultimate nature. For example, when awakening from dreamless sleep we will state that we lost consciousness. But which consciousness? Certainly the consciousness of time and space, but is that all there is to Consciousness? Yet we will say, "I was blissfully asleep" — we do not say "I was not there" while asleep. So something in us must have been aware of our Beingness during dreamless sleep. So even if we appear to be unconscious to the whole world — and I mean this in both senses, to ourselves and to others — Consciousness is ever there, because it is our inherent nature, in fact we are nothing else. And just because consciousness is always with us, we do not always notice. Let me give you an analogy. If you are in a room with a continuous low level of noise — so-called "white noise" — what happens after some time is that you do not notice the noise anymore. You appear to be in silence. Yet the real Silence becomes apparent only when the white noise is discontinued. Just so, one realizes the Consciousness as ever being one's true Self — the same state, both in deep sleep and in between incarnations — only when mind and body no longer intrude. Maybe, the overwhelmingly sensate values of our society act just like white noise in preventing us to recognize our real being.

Should we not study the brain, dualistic though such a study may be, in order to discover and understand better what is consciousness?

The scientific study of the brain is of interest to science; it is on the level of physiology and computer technology. The brain, like the mind, is really a sixth sense organ, a tool, helpful for physical survival, but nothing more. Consciousness uses the brain, expresses itself through it, but consciousness is not in the brain, the brain is in consciousness. So even if science were to achieve perfect knowledge of this organ, it would be no different than having perfect knowledge of the eye or ear — it would not bring man one iota closer to peace and fulfillment. So forget about the brain but inquire instead directly into consciousness, your real nature, how you actually function in duality — ever oscillating between the states of pleasure and pain, peace and turmoil — so that you may reach the non-state of "I am." Then that will give you a clue to all you have to know, and everything, all the blessings you need and that are your birthright, will become yours.

The best way for you to pursue this pathless path is not through research into science, which, as you rightly state, is thoroughly dualistic, but through your own meditation, your own inquiry, so that you may get the necessary insights first-hand and not from hearsay, and eventually a taste of the non-dual, the timeless, which alone is real.

2

Non-Duality Appears Counter-Intuitive to the Dualistic Mind

I don't get that feeling of "oneness" or non-duality you are talking about. On the contrary, from a young age I have been very conscious of my own uniqueness. My being, experience, knowledge of the world and my potential all seem to me highly individualistic. And I cannot imagine that a creator should have created something so special in order for it to be totally destroyed upon death of the body. I therefore believe that the soul is immortal. What do you say to that?

Although superficially many people feel a sense of uniqueness in their identity, to really discover one's own nature, one must go much deeper into the inquiry. Understand first that there is a commonality of thoughts, feelings and emotions in all mankind, in fact, all sentient beings — just as there is a commonality in the physical make-up of all humans since, broadly speaking, all have the same kind of heart, lungs, blood, etc. Thoughts and emotions do not come labeled with the person's identity; in truth, there is only thought, not X's thought or Y's thought, even though it may be expressed through body-mind "X" or body-mind "Y." The same consciousness imbues all creatures; only the expression is in accordance with the frame of reference of that creature. The sum total of all these thoughts and emotions derives from the collective consciousness, one's conditioning. All humanity is in you; there is nothing personal in us. You are the world! The concept of a "soul," uniquely one's own, is one of our most destructive illusions, because ultimately it is the cause of all psychological suffering. We cling to the idea, however, because without it we feel lost in emptiness. It is also for this reason that it is so hard to transcend the ego, born from the duality of the "me" and the "not-me."

For realizing the state of advaita, *to me the question is: to meditate or not to meditate. What do you recommend in this respect?*

It all depends what is meant by the term "meditation." If by "meditation" one means inquiry, or *vichara*, as it is called in the East, then meditation is highly desirable. The best and ultimate meditation is to meditate on the meditator, or "self-inquiry." But for perhaps the majority of people "meditation" implies something quite different. It is not inquiry that they are interested in, but some form of thought control, manipulation of the mind by the mind. They endeavor to mold the mind into some preapproved pattern, or to create a mind that is capable of doing all sorts of wonderful and extraordinary things, a mind with great powers or *siddhis*. Now, in themselves, there is nothing wrong with such efforts, only it has nothing to do with realizing the state of *advaita*, the ultimate freedom.

To work on the mind by the mind can only lead to one's becoming more entrenched in duality. We must realize that all such efforts take place within thought, within the mind. They depend upon one's creation of and adherence to various concepts. The primary concept is that of an "I," the idea that one is something, rather than the truth that one is Empty or Nothing, which goes beyond even the concepts of emptiness or nothingness.

Advaita is totally free from concepts because it lies beyond the mind, body and senses. At the same time, it must be clearly recognized that any action at all, whether on the worldly or the spiritual level, is not possible without some form of conceptualization. I cannot begin to meditate without some idea about myself as the meditator, and the result will ever only be a movement within thought. Thus, the only sure way towards *advaita* is simply to keep quiet. This may appear simple, but for most of us it has become excruciatingly difficult and painful. Yet this is the chief message of the Indian sage, Poonjaji: Let the mind fall silent and then see what happens. One will find that what remains is pure Existence, Consciousness or Bliss (*satchitananda*).

Is a so-called "intellectual" search a help or a hindrance?

Find out what comprises the intellect and then you will know about its being a help or a hindrance. But let me just say that the intellectual search has legitimacy only in the beginning, since at that point that is all you have at your disposal. The intellect or mind must be turned inward before one can discover anything of value. But it is not the intellect that can do the spiritual exploration.

The mind must be directed towards its matrix and see its own relativity and thereby its own ultimate unreality and irrelevancy in the quest. In this connection, this is the only function of the intellect — to undo itself by discovering its own limitations for the task in hand — not to actually discover anything new. Anything the intellect discovers is of its own conditioning and therefore of the old; it can never step beyond its own boundaries. But once the intellect realizes that — its own impotence in the spiritual quest, its own irrelevancy — it gets out of the way. It may not want to do so easily and at first will create a lot of fuss, but eventually it will have to give up. That constitutes the real transcendence, and at that point the Real always manifests in and through its own splendor.

Why does advaita *allow for diversity on the manifest level?*

Sri Nisargadatta Maharaj explains this by analogy with the mother who has ten children, each different — the result of many combinations and permutations (of the five elements). The manifest level is the *Mayaic* level; it reflects reality but is not reality itself. Another well-known and often quoted analogy in this connection is the following: Gold ever remains as gold, even though it may be molded into a thousand different shapes as rings, pendants and other forms of "jewelry." Multiplicity or diversity is therefore more a matter of perception, seeing, than of ontology; what *is* is ever true unicity.

I find that the idea of advaita *does not come easily to me. I don't experience non-duality as natural, whereas I do feel that with duality. If duality is false and non-duality is the truth, should not my feelings be the exact opposite?*

As long as we entertain *advaita* as an idea, this "strangeness" will persist. You see, "idea" means "thought" is involved as an intermediary, and thought itself is already dualistic. Without duality there can be no thought. So if you investigate this matter by means of thought, everything will be tainted by duality. It is like looking at the world through colored glasses: inevitably, the world assumes the color of your glasses. If you want to find out the true color of the world, you must throw away your glasses or use clear ones. Just so with this question of non-duality; if you want to discover this for yourself, you must throw away the tool of thought. Go to a place where thought does not reign. For example, when dreamlessly asleep, you are fully immersed in the state of non-duality without even a tinge of duality. Does it still feel unnatural? This is your natural state! The same freedom from duality is also experienced in the interval between thoughts, and in the short moment after waking up from deep sleep. To be aware of the naturally peaceful and blissful condition of the deep-sleep state even while fully awake — *jagrat-sushupti* — is the highest state and was attained and continuously lived by Sri Ramana Maharshi.

More generally, your question raises the problem of whether intuition can always be relied upon in one's search for the truth. This applies even within the field of duality. For example, time was in physics when one could rely upon common-sense observation, such as the experience of seeing the sun rise and set and one therefore concluded that the sun revolves around the earth. Now we know this to be erroneous, only because of more sophisticated means of instrumentation, and that the truth is the exact opposite.

Another example is that matter was experienced as fully solid and even after the introduction of the atomic model, one was dealing with small particles having a variety of fairly familiar properties such as mass and electrical charge. This has now changed fundamentally with the arrival of the so-called "new physics." Particles are no longer seen as "solid," but are considered equivalent to energy and electromagnetic waves. Some have properties that are so outlandish that physicists use the concept of "strangeness" for an established physical parameter. Thus, the era of "intuitive understanding," at least in modern physics, is over.

More generally, I would suggest there are two kinds of intuition, which might be called the lower and higher intuition. Lower intuition is that which applies in the world of duality, a rapid unrehearsed understanding that quickly comes to the point. This understanding still takes place in a dualistic frame of reference involving thought and concept. Higher intuition is the discovery of truths on the most fundamental level, particularly as they apply to self-discovery, where reason no longer plays any role (which does not mean, however, that one has become irrational!).

So what all this signifies is that the ordinary intuition which is inherent in most of us can be valid for understanding the coarser phenomena on the dualistic level. The higher kind of intuition must be developed as one matures spiritually and is the only instrument at one's disposal for the discovery of the subtlest phenomena leading eventually to the ultimate reality.

A parallel is found in the teachings of Sri Atmananda (Krishna Menon). He distinguishes between lower reason and higher reason, where lower reason is ordinary thought or logic, and by higher reason is meant the intuition required to perceive spiritual truths.

To sum up, the commonsense point of view by which many things are felt naturally as being correctly defined and which can be visualized intuitively might be a reasonable pointer in our wanderings through a familiar world, dualistically. But it is not necessarily the best tool on the more refined levels of thought and feeling and definitely not on the ultimate level, where thought has to be left behind if one wishes to reach the Supreme.

3

MAYA IS A STAGE IN OUR UNDERSTANDING

If one seriously engages in meditation or self-inquiry, it will be found that there is a superficial layer of consciousness, which consists of thoughts and patterns of thought, all based on memories and so, ultimately, on impressions and experiences. The continuous flow of these thoughts leads us to believe in the existence of a functional organ called "mind." But actually the mind has no existence in itself apart from the flow of thoughts. The nature of these thoughts exhibits certain patterns, which signify and assure the continuity of the "flow." This self-serving and self-preserving mode of the thought flow is called "ego."

The thought patterns appear on the consciousness, as waking and sleeping, just like the flowing of the tides manifests on the Ocean. Again, the actual nature of the thoughts is Consciousness only, which is the changeless element among the changeful, and therefore the real, the Self. Below the level of thought, or perhaps it is better stated as "prior to it," is the awareness or attention level which, though itself changeless, can perceive the ever changeful thoughts, emotions, feelings, etc. — our everyday travail. This deeper level of consciousness can potentially witness the movements of the mind. By virtue of its pure witnessing, i.e., impersonal observation without involvement in what is observed, it can neutralize the tyranny of the "personal." This witness activity gives us an intimation of the Self, which is beyond all travail, and is the gateway toward Liberation. The "witness," however, is not the Self itself, but is the purest representation or manifestation of it on the level of mind.

Thus, the Self is the permanent background of the transient manifestation of thoughts, emotions, feelings, etc. Therefore, seen from the superficial point of view of the impositions or the *Maya* of the changeful, the underlying reality of the changeless or "is-ness" is as Nothing, because it lies outside any subject-object relationship and so is beyond the possibility of perception. Therefore, the ignorant will assign the attribute of "nonexistence" to it. But as we have already shown, the very concept of "Nothingness" in the nihilistic sense can exist only for the ignorant.

Having perceived and understood all this, I know that my real nature is not affected by space and time, just as the Ocean itself is not affected by the tides: "I am," regardless of "when" and "where," which means my real nature is eternal and infinite. That is, it is beyond existence and nonexistence, beyond the realm where things can happen to me — beyond "happeness," as it were, and therefore beyond both happiness and unhappiness. The state, or better, "non-state" may best be designated as "peace," "bliss," or "realization."

What is the best way to attain non-duality?

Ultimately, there is no "best way" and there are no well-defined recipes to that effect, no easy lessons in enlightenment that can be learned in a short period of time. There is only one way, to realize one's mistaken identity with the body-mind. All approaches for the beginner are only preludes and incentives meant to lead us to that essential search. If you sincerely want to realize your self, then tackle that issue of your identity as the foremost priority. Cease being the individual you have imagined yourself to be all these years. All other issues pale into insignificance compared with the fundamental search "Who am I?"

How can I accept that we are not our bodies when clearly we all have a body for the whole world to see?

You may have a body, just as you may, for example, have a book, but that does not mean that you *are* that body, just as you are not that book. In fact, when you say that you have a body, does not that immediately imply that you are inherently different from it, certainly much greater or more fundamental?

But even when saying that we have a body, on a deeper level that may not be correct either. For what is that "we"? "We" implies a multitude of "I"s, and has one been able to concretize that "I"? Therefore, does not the uttering of that term "we," ultimately imply identification with some entity? Unless one is absolutely clear on the nature of that "we" the statement cannot have any meaning. It is merely a self-affirming uttering, for that "we" as we use the term means only some structure or concept associated with a certain body. Otherwise, "we" or "I" could not have arisen. Thus, in the phrasing of the problem we are already affirming something that is still being explored, still in need of definition, a kind of circular argument — in other words, we are begging the question!

The trouble is that we have long forgotten that moment in the distant past when we first uttered consciously the words "I am," inaugurating a long period of living from a point of view of "I"-ness. This state of being will then find its apotheosis through the ripening of understanding, when one can consciously utter the magic words "I am that I am," and one's actions are freed from the previously existing narrow focus of self-interest.

Similarly, with regard to acceptance of the existence of "body," the truth is that on the most fundamental level, there is not even a "body," as conventionally envisaged. The term is merely a shorthand expression for some familiar concept associated with a fairly constant experience or impression. What applies when using the term "we" applies equally when using the term "body." Yes, body certainly exists as "appearance," but no, beyond this superficial appearance, body does not exist at all. "Body" is actually a gross impression of our sense organs, which because of its familiarity is taken for granted. Hence, we think we know what we mean when we use that term "body," but we actually do not. What lies behind this sensory appearance is something much grander, much more fundamental, and totally beyond our wildest conceptualization.

Like yourself, many teachers of advaita *have stated that the emergence of an ego, the cause of man's basic ignorance and suffering, is the result of the consciousness identifying itself with a body. Understanding this fully would therefore give us a mighty key to liberation. However, exactly how this identification works is not spelled out, and I would like therefore to know in more detail the* modus operandi *of this mechanism.*

You are asking me what is perhaps the $64,000 question of spirituality!

The way I view it is that once linkage between the self and a particular body has been established, it is not too difficult to see that such identification is reinforced every time there is a reactivation of existing engrams of body-wise or body-related memories.

But it is more difficult to understand how this linkage takes place in the first place, the birth of a virgin "I" or ego, as it were, through the primordial identification or association of consciousness with the body. For it would be through this process that the original engrams or *samskaras* are established.

Here, the question may not even be a legitimate one. You see, one may visualize the association of two discrete entities, but Consciousness is all-embracing — there is nothing beside itSelf. So in actual fact, the Self would be identifying with itself, which makes nonsense of the question, since identification, by definition, can occur only between entities that are different and separate from each other.

The basic question to my mind is how this original feeling of a "me" comes about — the "me" which lies at the heart of practically everything I do in my mental and physical activities. Now it seems there are two possibilities here. First, the "I" comes about initially within consciousness and then identifies with a particular body. In other words, a psychological entity, the mind or ego, comes about through some unknown event or mechanism, which then attaches itself to a particular body. I believe this is how Sri Ramana Maharshi saw it. He stated that the "I"-thought, or the germ of the little self, arises from the Self or the Heart, and the clue to liberation lies in tracing that "I"-thought back to the Self.

The second possibility is the following. Awareness detects little change in my body appearance from day to day, and so the consciousness, ever recognizing an *approximately* constant body image, brings about a localized mind, as it were, around such a body center — the "I" or ego. In other words, through this very identification, a psychological center is brought about.

In recapitulation, in the first case, the "me" is born within Consciousness before identification with a body takes place (although such identification may take place well after the body's birth.). In other words, there is an existing "me" that seeks out and identifies with a body. In the second case, the "me" emerges only *as the result of* such identification. Many people, including myself at one time, did accept the second explanation as the correct one. Now, however, I do not hold with that anymore. There are several reasons for this, the main one of which is perhaps the following: Identification implies exclusivity. And the term "me" is virtually synonymous with exclusivity. So why should consciousness at any one moment select an individual body-entity to identify with, when there are untold billions of such bodies? And if, in fact, it identifies itself with a multitude of body-entities, then I am not sure whether the concept of identification still has any meaning.

Furthermore, there are the following arguments that militate against the latter hypothesis. Upon waking in the morning from deep sleep, it is actually possible to experience for oneself this birth of the "I." Sooner or later, we become aware of our identity even while still having our eyes closed. We don't need to inspect and recognize our bodies to be convinced as to who we are!

A small child develops his personal identity only after some time, perhaps one to two years. If the "I" consciousness were purely a matter of the consciousness recognizing the body, then the child's identity would have been present immediately after his sense organs became functional. But it appears that identification of a psychological "me" with a body occurs well into the development of the infant. (Incidentally, I don't know whether this has any relevance to the abortion debate.)

Further, as we already stated, from the ultimate point of view, these so-called extraneous body-entities are in fact nonexistent, since everything exists only within consciousness and that is all that exists. They are no more than *Mayaic* will-o'-the-wisps.

To end this discussion, I no longer feel the original question is a valid one. My view is that the way in which the problem was originally phrased, namely, the identification of consciousness with a body, is more a figure of speech than actual description of events. Rather than an identification, we should see it as a "crystallization" of a psychological center, the "me," within consciousness. Then, to ask why or how this crystallization takes place is not a valid question. There is no why or how in truly fundamental matters; causality no longer applies on this level. It is a primordial event, which is its own cause and is only another aspect of the question how and why *Maya* arose. After all, outside the Consciousness, nothing has reality — it is all *Maya*. In fact, it is exactly the same problem in different words.

Finally, somewhat related to this question, I would like to make the following observations. Within the realm of *Maya*, I view the body as having its own special form of protective consciousness, though of a lower order — largely as memory and therefore mechanically, physiologically, reactive. And similarly, the individual cells have their own protective consciousness contained in their DNA, and possibly down to the quantum level. And I see this same pattern in all biological systems, from the simplest unicellular organisms to the most complex forms of life as in humans. These lower consciousnesses we are talking about are purely somatic and non-psychological. They are present also in the more evolved expressions of life, but there, in addition, the Self touches the somatic bases and thereby introduces a psychological component in the form of a "me."

Is it true what some people say, that it is easier for a person with a strong ego to realize himself than for one with a weak ego?

Yes and no. Intrinsically, it is no different; the process of transcendence remains the same. But it so happens that the throbbing of a strong ego is likely to make more waves and so elicit more attention than that of a weaker one, both within and without. It is very much like hearing an annoying noise in one's car. When it is a weak one, or intermittent, it is much more difficult to detect its exact location and cause. Not infrequently, the mechanic will advise us to wait until the noise has become somewhat worse and steadier; then it will be much easier for him to diagnose and fix the problem.

Similarly, the waves of disturbance emanating from a strong ego are a strong call for investigation. Thus, the "owner" of such an ego is at one time or another likely to take note of the "noise" that his ego machinery is making; he simply can no longer ignore it. At such a time, the individual has become painfully aware of his own existence, causing him to direct his attention inwardly. Incidentally, his situation is similar to that of the person who throughout his life has been dealt a bad hand by fate. Probably no greater incentive to "waking up" and exploring the inner life exists than suffering, and maybe one can see this fact as a way of divine compensation!

Up to this point, all the individual had been doing was blaming various outside causes for his recurring crises. If he is of a sensible disposition, he will naturally first want to find the cause of that which is constantly getting him in trouble. If he persists in his examination or "meditation" — and the incentive is surely there if the crisis is frequent and acute enough — he will eventually find out that the disturbance emanates from the confluence of both external and internal sources. This will signal to him that there must also be something radically wrong with the percipient himself. Ultimately, pursuing the investigation to the very end, he will come to the conclusion that on the most fundamental level he as an individual is wholly the cause of the mental pain. This realization is concomitant with the understanding that the outer and the inner are not separate; the individual is the world and comprises the entire field of consciousness. Through this insight, he realizes that, strangely, he is simultaneously the recipient (as the experiencer) and the creator of the discomfort. But having created it, he can reverse the mental process which he has so carefully observed and finally understood, and thereby "uncreate" the pain. This is truly a marvelous discovery since it points up at once the way out of psychological suffering.

What is the meaning of Maya?

Maya, in its most fundamental meaning, signifies that the world as perceived by the senses and the mind does not really exist as such. It is not only a matter of not trusting the accuracy of one's sense perception, which is very susceptible to misperception of all kinds, but to doubt its deeper meaning or interpretation. You see, perception does not necessarily prove the reality of the world of objects. What, in this connection, is an "object"? An object is, if nothing else, "form." It may also announce itself through any of the other senses. Therefore, we can state that objects are purely form, sound, taste, smell, and tactile sensation; they cannot by any stretch of the imagination be divorced from the corresponding sense organs. Furthermore, these sense functions can in turn not be divorced from consciousness. It is consciousness that gives them light and life; otherwise, these functions are only potential, not actual. In sum, objects as such, existing in their own right, do not exist; the controversial "Ding an sich" (Thing in itself) is a figment of the imagination.

This can also be understood in a slightly different way. When we talk about an object, we refer to an entity with definite boundaries or interfaces in space and time. Now these delimitations are arbitrarily assigned by the observer, based on his own capacities, his own particular makeup as an observer-object. An object is perceived by the light it reflects. Here, the visual characteristics observed for the object are dependent on and limited by the physical characteristics of the observer. The eye is receptive only within a particular range of the electromagnetic wave spectrum; anything that falls outside it is not registered and does not therefore exist for it. Night goggles use infrared, invisible to the human eye, and these rays therefore have to be converted to a shorter wavelength to be perceptible to the human eye. A bat can observe in total darkness by using sound waves, it "sees" acoustically. Such examples show us that what is perceived — its quality and contents — is quite arbitrary and as much a function of the observer as of the observed. We can therefore state that there are no inherent properties of the object that make it into an independently existing entity. More properly, it can be said that the object is a reflection of the senses and the mind.

In short, observer and object are not discontinuous, but as has been expressed: the observer *is* the observed, the "subject" is the "object." In other words, the entire operational field of experience is one continuum; this represents the essential truth of *advaita* (non-duality). Having thus transcended all boundaries, the objects have now disappeared from existence. Being arbitrarily projected, they are unreal or *Maya*. All that can be measured is measurable only in the field of *avidya*, ignorance.

The close interdependence between observer and object applies similarly to the psychological aspects of observer and object. A situation (here, the situation is the "object") attractive to one observer may be of no interest or even distasteful to another observer. Again, there are no absolutes in the cognitive process. The proclivities of the observer — that is, his whole psychological background or conditioning — color or mold the observation; no "situation" exists on its own. The observer and the observed are not separate realities but form one continuum.

How does Maya *come into being?*

I can't tell you how it primordially arose as the "world" and "ego," but I can tell you how subsequently it continually arises and is maintained. First, because of comparison — the "I" entity is maintained that way. Second, because of sentimentality. The memories of past images of "I" are cherished and protected, as though they are something tangible and not just dead images of the past. And third, the network of thought with its recurring patterns, easily recognized, constantly reinforces the unreal entity.

I have some difficulty with the cavalier manner in which you relegate time and space to the unreal. To me, they represent the most tangible foundations of Existence. Whatever is *seems to be built on these very real parameters. How can you say so lightly that all that is nothing but* Maya*?*

Because you add the words "to me," there is some truth in your statement about space and time being the most tangible foundations. But this is just where the shoe pinches, because to say baldly "space and time are the foundation stones of Existence" would be totally false;

Existence is something much grander than any structure built from space-time. The key to the riddle lies entirely in the words "*To me.*" What is that "me" and what role does it play in viewing the world and what we call "Existence"? Without further defining and understanding that "me" or the observer, the observation surely has no significance. If one looks at the world through tinted glasses and one does not know that simple fact, then surely whatever I say about the tints of the world has no meaning whatsoever, since I myself have superimposed these attributes on the world.

Visualize now that instead of tints we are dealing with space-time. Analogously to the above example, I am looking at Existence through a structure consisting of space-time. Put in a few words, it can be said that in the dualistic view, in which each one of us is a separate entity, space-time is the universal matrix of the "known." The very meaning of "knowing" and the "known" implies putting things into a space-time frame of reference, whether we look at things in the most simplistic, everyday way of "experiencing" or through the most sophisticated and exalted concept, such as Einstein's, where space-time is seen as a curvature in what we experience as and call "matter."

Now as soon as any observation is described or any thought is expressed, underlying such a statement is the word "I." "I" indicates a restriction and means that one has set oneself apart from something else, expressing oneself as something, as a "being" in contradistinction from Beingness or "I-am-ness." This being or creature, upon further "development," is then called "individuality" or "personality."

Upon the first stirring of thought, as on waking up from deep sleep, a certain orientation in the field of consciousness comes about, or perhaps better: a "field" is created overlaying the pure non-field of consciousness or sentience, which is the state — or non-state — liberated from content. Thus, *Advaita* has got lost in the shuffle, through the various mind noises. And now the world miraculously appears *dvaitic* or dualistic: caught by *Maya*, as *Maya*! Much like a mirage . . . Prior to all this happening, one obviously was, and essentially still is, nondivided or the Totality. Now how can space exist for the Totality? Space originally is based on the concept that we can go from point A to point B, but for one who is the totality this is unimaginable, there is no coming or going, no "here" or "there"! It would be like the ocean questioning the whereabouts of water.

Similarly with time. Time is based on movement, and movement naturally presupposes space. So first of all, in a reality devoid of space, how could one visualize "movement" and secondarily "time"? In a world without movement, either physical or mental, could the concept of time even arise? How could there be movement for something that is at once everywhere, complete, perfect within itSelf? Can we not see that a break must be made with our old ways of thinking, spatially and temporally, which are now seen to be a creation of our faulty premise, that we are fractions and not the Whole? Perhaps more succinctly put: Is not our very first thought the seed of all error, all that which is implied in the concept

"I" or "self"? Always remember, therefore: Before Concept, before the Word, the "Self" is.

I can see some truth in what you say about space and time, since these are purely abstract categories, but surely this does not apply to "matter"? How can anyone deny reality to matter, for which we have solid evidence from our sense organs? Connected with this is my problem with a statement you made in the past that the body per se does not really exist and that all is Mind or Consciousness.

The difference between you and me is that I don't take the evidence of the sense organs as the final arbiter in the matter (no pun intended!). The sense organs are also "matter" and how can like prove the existence of like? The final evaluation of any sensory input is always in and through consciousness. When that final receptor is temporarily unavailable, such as in deep sleep, what evidence for the existence of matter, or of anything for that matter, do I have?

The complex of sense organs cum central nervous system can give me all kinds of information, but what does it actually mean? All of it is still on the level of impressions, appearances, *Maya* if you like, and it never goes beyond this level. It is the same complex that produces all kinds of dreams while asleep, but on waking we know they were just pictures and impressions, and nothing more. Just so, we should regard our sense impressions during the waking state.

But even on a grosser level, things don't add up for those who so readily trust the evidence of their senses. A moment ago I did refer to Einstein's conclusion that matter can be reduced to a curvature of space-time, which means that essentially matter *is* space-time. So if you can accept what was said in relation to space-time, then all that would hold true for matter also.

Finally, we must always keep in mind that things are not what they seem at first impression. All the familiar attributes of what we call "matter," such as mass, solidity, energy, spatial dimensions, etc., have been thrown in doubt by physicists who have explored matter in depth. They have found that for the very smallest particles of which all matter seems to be composed these familiar properties no longer apply. Thus, in sub-fundamental-particle size, it is obviously impossible to go on describing properties in terms of the particles themselves, just as it is impossible for a knife cutting itself or an eye seeing itself. Again, one might say that the unknown cannot be expressed in terms of the known.

I think the concept of Maya *is just a cop-out, to lend some kind of justification to the philosophy of* advaita *without which it would be clearly untenable — since all human experience is obviously dualistic, and, in fact, no experience is even possible without duality.*

Let's look at it in stages. In first instance, *Maya* means simply "illusion"; on a deeper level, it means "that which is to be measured," a distinct reference to that which can be fixed within a space-time frame of reference. According to the first definition, when you state that *Maya* does not exist, at least for you, the implication is that you are perfect. For is it not a fact that all our perceptions and conceptions are subject to error, and so to illusion? Most of us fall into the trap of seeing the proverbial snake in the rope, most of the time! So to state that *Maya* is nonexistent for you makes you into a god, infallible.

As to *Maya* according to the second definition, anything that can be measured comprises the full range of human experience, all that is in space-time, the entire world of "objects" — the cosmos. It all depends on one's point of view. From the point of view of the individual observer, there are obviously discrete entities in space and time. The messages the senses receive continually signal the existence of objects to the observer. From a broader perspective or a higher point of view, however, the observer himself is an object, too, even though he regards himself as the subject. This observer objectifies everything within his field of experience, but is ignorant or forgetful of the background against which these objects appear. Yet, that background is indispensable, for without it no objects could be known. It must be concluded that the background is the primary reality; the objects are appearances, just as the rope appears as a snake. In the latter case, I see a snake with my own eyes, yet there is no such thing at all. When I look more closely I discover my error: the snake (object) no longer appears, only the rope (background) is there. Thus, perception does not prove that an object exists.

The objects appear and disappear, but what is ever there is the background, the awareness, in which manifestation takes place. No objects, as we said, can exist without awareness, but awareness can exist without objects, such as is the case in deep sleep. In that state, no objects appear, yet on waking we have retained the sense of identity with our real nature; if the awareness were cut off, we would not have that sense of continuity of being. Thus, awareness being eternal, outside the field of space and time, nothing external to it can exist; it is therefore the only reality and so must be identical with our Self. All the rest — the objects and concepts based on them— are therefore said to be *Maya.*

You say that the observer, though regarding himself the subject, is actually only an object among objects. I don't see it that way: I perceive the objects but the objects don't see me; therefore, I am the subject.

That is correct on the level of *Maya*, but only on that superficial level. On a deeper level, one must understand what is the so-called object and what is the observer. The object is always perceived against a background of space; we say it "occupies" space. Without space there cannot be an object, but without object there still is the space. So analogously to our previous reasoning: the object appears on a background of space and, within this particular context, only the space is primordial, and the object is *Maya* in relation to the space. Here it must always be remembered that there exist several levels of unreality, but there is only one level of reality. Now, even the space is still on the level of unreality or *Maya*, because in itself it is an object to the perceiver, the body-mind entity. And the latter, having come about through identification with the body, which is an object, is thereby itself objectified, so it cannot have absolute reality. Then, who or what, in this context, is the Ultimate Perceiver? The final background in which all perceptions are received or "apperceived" is the consciousness or awareness, which is therefore the only true and ultimate Subject or, perhaps more appropriately, Subjectivity itself. Now since all objects find their being in that consciousness — that is, everything is part of the windows, which is the totality — it is as true to state that the objects see me as that I see the objects!

To me, however, the major question remains: Who exactly is the seer?

Because we come up with different pictures of the world, we think there is a multitude of seers. Actually, there is only one seer; the different pictures are only different interpretations of the world. One way to understand this is by visualizing the one seer as separated from the world by a multitude of windows, whereby each window manages to open up to or "see" a different world. What actually happens is that each window supplies its own distortion or *maya* to the seen. Yet again, each of these individual renditions of what *is* is a mere aspect of a universal distortion or *Maya*. Now what are the windows composed of that they give rise to this effect of individuation or illusion? They are the specificities of body-mind characteristics plus the "history" — that is, the integral experience or conditioning through culture and genetic inheritance of each body-mind entity. The latter can also be said to be the *samskaras* which have given rise to a set of *vasanas*. Whose set of *vasanas*? Nobody's! The *vasanas* are just that, pure energy packages of potential desire unsatisfied. One can visualize this by thinking of the potential energy preserved in a stretched-out elastic band. It will always want to return to its original contracted state or rest position. Similarly, desire ever wishes for its gratification in order to return to a state of balance or rest, in which the desire is not. Thus, these *vasanas* must be seen as independent concentrations of energy that persist through time, independent of the persistence of the body-mind entity with which they are temporarily associated. As Nisargadatta Maharaj has said, there is a rebirth of sorts, but it is not the same individual that is reborn.

In some of your books you seem to differentiate between the terms consciousness and Consciousness (spelled with a capital C). What is the difference?

The former has content; Consciousness has not because it is not confined within a subject-object relationship. Consciousness (with a capital C) knows no continuity, as it is beyond space-time; consciousness is essentially continuity, being confined to space-time.

Matters of life and death can only be discussed within the realm of consciousness, because they center around a body-mind entity; Consciousness transcends both life and death and refers, therefore, to our eternal nature — That which exists before our so-called birth and after our so-called "death" and even in our present "embodiment."

Whereas Consciousness does not depend on anything beyond Itself but everything depends on It, consciousness is always found in association with a body. Consciousness is the Absolute, and consciousness reflects the state of the relative, the body-mind sphere.

4

Death is Feared Because It is Not Understood

You have spoken about the importance of coming to grips with the fear of death. But what would you say to someone like myself who has had a happy and completely fulfilled life and is not yet ready to part with all of that? Is fear of death not fully justified in my circumstances?

I say that the fear of death is completely misplaced, even on your present level of understanding, if you would just investigate the matter for yourself. We spend so much of our energy throughout life affirming our appearance yet devote so little energy to investigating how this appearance has come about, which might give us a clue to our eventual but certain disappearance. But it is the very fear that prevents you from looking more deeply. Let me put it most succinctly: The fear of death comes into being when the anchor of "*self*-ness" (not "selfish-ness", that comes later) descends into the soil of "is-ness" and gets stuck there. Prevent this fear from being born by not letting this "self"-ness take root in the first place. That is the only radical solution, and is the clue to every other problem in consciousness.

When death arrives, it is like a thief in the night. The body stops functioning, the vital air mingles with the universal air, and consequently all capacity for perception and experience comes to an end. It is like falling asleep. Does one fear falling asleep? No, on the contrary, we all look forward to a good night's sleep. And the pertinent point is that we never experience the transition from waking to sleep. That moment is unknown and unknowable, because to know it one has to be awake. *The individual never knows what is happening to him!* For the simple reason that the individual, who while the body is there, has at best a ghostlike existence, now no longer even has that pseudo existence and is completely gone. So who is there to experience death?

My answer therefore is that you have nothing to lose, nothing to fear from death. And if this is so for you who have been reasonably content with existence, what about that person whose bodily existence is nothing but suffering? Indeed, he actually stands to gain, for the deletion of a negative is actually a positive: the liberation from all that pain. In a sense, death for him represents an immense blessing. This person will only benefit from becoming insentient, for the period of his suffering will be mercifully reduced. It is like having the ideal analgesic, one without side effects!

Essentially, to fear death is a contradiction in terms, for we can only fear a concept, a projection from the present into the future; it is never the actuality, which in this case is death itself. Another way to put the problem is as follows: living in or with the body brings about functioning in time. Fear is a product of time, a form of time actually, and so long as the body is operational we function in time. But the moment the body drops away, we cease to function in time and so the "I" or the experiencer is lost. In short, contrary to popular opinion, we shall never "know death," just as we never knew "birth."

I have dealt with the problem from the point of view of someone who still holds to his "personhood." Once this plane of functioning has been transcended and all the false images and concepts which memory has tricked us into accepting have been seen through, the question of death never arises anymore. One then already lives intimately with death, even though the body is still functional and therefore the capacity for experience has not yet been lost. It is the inevitable result of letting go of everything, upon the realization that the division of the "I" and the "non-I" is false and that life and death form one continuum, making fear irrelevant. Then all the minor and major aims and goals that I have been pursuing no longer hold any fascination and therefore drop away by themselves. I am totally nothingness in a world of nothingness: I no longer live but am being lived. At that point, the affirmation of one's appearance into the manifest dynamic consciousness has been transcended and transmuted into the acknowledgment of one's impending disappearance. I no longer hold on to anything nor reject anything. A new question then blossoms forth spontaneously and miraculously: "What am I still doing in this world?" This question, however, does not require any answer, but what matters only is the *feeling* inducing the question.

You talk about man's immortality, an insight that you seem to have gained through meditation and contemplation. Do you think the time will ever come that immortality can be proved scientifically, for everyone to see and accept?

It will never happen. First of all, if such a thing were possible, don't you think that man has been around long enough for such a rational demonstration to have happened already? But the real point is this: What is to prove man's immortality? It is only body, mind and senses that could do so. And body, mind and senses are themselves ephemeral, transient. Now can the ephemeral prove the eternal? It is not logically possible. In fact — and this is a subtle point — it is just the other way around: It is the very fact of man's eternal nature that has made it possible to recognize the ephemeral nature of body, mind and senses. Were it not for his eternal base, man would not know anything.

But another question should be asked: Why is there this continual demand for proof of man's immortality? Why is it that we cannot live with what we are in the here and now, without the assurance of eternal life? Why cannot the psychosomatic entity live in a transient world? The transient will always long to give itself continuity, which is in the nature of things. It imagines that to be security. But the root of the problem is that this so-called "psychosomatic entity" has never examined itself sufficiently. Although it feels as though it is an entity, it is actually a process and that only as a first approximation. When one goes more deeply into it, even this "process" is seen to be not that but really the Totality, the Emptiness, or, paradoxically, the fullness beyond space and time. The recognition of that fullness brings fulfillment and wipes away all insecurity, all demand for something else.

You probably know that there are still people in this world who believe that in due course physical immortality — that is, unlimited life extension — may be achieved through various means. They suggest it may be possible to let the body live forever, perhaps by manipulation of the genetic code or by continual transplantation of the vital organs, or perhaps through high-velocity space travel. If science could achieve such a feat, would it not undercut all spiritual endeavor?

Ah, shades of Paracelsus and the ancient alchemists in their search for the philosopher's stone! And I am well aware of current thinking that, according to Einstein's Relativity theory, humans would indeed experience a time-dilation effect and thereby be able to achieve life extension. However, I view all such maneuvers still in the realm of thought experiments and riddled with paradox. But above all, I must stress that even if life extension through any such means were to become fact, it would still only be stretching the life span and not physical immortality. Mankind would still find itself short of

Infinity. Over the past decades medical advances and improvement in the living conditions have extended the life span in certain parts of the world considerably, yet has this changed anything in our fear of death? Even if a man were to live a thousand years, this fear would still be his constant companion.

But let us look for one moment at the imaginary situation in which bodily immortality has become an actuality: You are then destined to live forever. What a horrible fate: a life sentence, from which no escape is possible . . . something like the man who has never slept and for some physiological reason is unable to sleep ever. This analogy is not wholly imaginary, since a few cases of the latter condition are known to medical science. But perhaps worst of all: Self-realization would become all that more difficult to achieve. Man would find it almost impossible to distinguish between finite and infinite values! The persistence in the life of the objects would blind us even more to the unchanging background from which all objects have sprung. To have the body present everlastingly would make it all that much more difficult to wean ourselves from identification with the body, and accordingly, the mind's regime also would be all that much more oppressive. Overall, our present difficulty in differentiating between appearance and reality would be accentuated and *Maya*'s reign would be strengthened.

You see, most of us live from a baseline that extends from birth. From being nothing, we suddenly become something material and mental, and all life is a process of hanging on to and developing this tangible atom that has sprung from a zero baseline. Consciously or unconsciously, we push away the absolutely certain destination of an imaginary entity that one has identified with. I view my life from the opposite end, from a zero baseline at death backwards to birth, which I feel ever keeps me on my toes and much more in touch with what *is*. It constantly reinforces the total evanescence of everything about me. It makes it that much less likely for me to build up false security in any aspect of my body-mind configuration.

When it comes to material things, all of us quite naturally keep in mind the limited life span of things that we build and handle; all financial thinking is imbued with the necessity to write off equipment and products over a certain period. Why do we forget this practical wisdom when it comes to our own body-mind systems? Constantly keeping in mind the inevitable end, the dissolution of one's system, one will in effect be using a different baseline and thereby staying closer to the Reality which runs from Nothingness to Nothingness. When my whole thinking is oriented in this factual manner, it will be that much easier to realize my essential nature as Nothingness even in the intervening period between both baselines.

Why is it that I cannot rid myself of the fear of death?

Ask yourself why do you want to go on living? Can you point to anything tangible you are gaining by so-called living? Before you were born with this body, were you afraid of death? No? Why then are you afraid now? Since the only thing that has changed is the appearance of a body, why should that make any difference to you? Don't blame the body. After all, it is nothing more than a corpse, an animated mass of cells, in itself insentient. Unless you identify yourself with it, why should you be concerned? You, in your self, in your real nature, are eternal and the only thing that matters. You are the living principle without which that body would be worthless. The "you" is the awareness of "I am," or the Beingness, signaled through your body, senses and mind. It is also through the body that your essence is manifested in space-time, but that essence itself is infinite — that is, it transcends space — as well as timeless or eternal. So first know the knower, that which you truly are, then see whether there is still any fear of death.

If I am really equal to Infinity, why am I in a finite and painful world?

Because we have refused to be Infinity, we have identified ourselves with finite and transient things, our minds are filled with trivialities, and by and large, our actions are based on petty concepts. Therefore we must suffer the consequences of being insignificant playthings, destined only to being pushed around and trampled upon. As long as all our values are based on the finite and therefore limited, how can we claim to be infinite and expect to partake of our birthright, the essentially pure and blissful state of being?

What is the Emptiness?

Find out: Is there anything that you can call wholly your own, indisputably and permanently? Obviously, it is not the body or anything bodily, since the body is continuously in flux. This becomes very obvious when one sees that the person as represented by the body now is something entirely different from the person say twenty years ago or immediately after birth. Similarly with the mind, which is continuously gathering new impressions and new memories, and dropping old ones. Owing to this continuous change, the eternal flux, the so-called "person" is different from moment to moment, and it is only our false perception that credits that person with a permanent identity. The world outside our skin is similarly in a state of continuous flux. Our conclusion is that there is nothing lasting, either within the skin or outside it, and so nothing can be said to have self-nature.

The same applies to values one tries to live by; these are relative to time and place and circumstances. What is "good" in one place and at one time may be "bad" in another place and at another time. The totality of this insight is known as the experience of Emptiness, as one has absolutely nothing to hold on to, no absolute values to live by: There is only living from moment to moment with what *is.* Most people find this very unsettling and frightening, but it is only so when one has been brought up to accept one's faulty, superficial impression of the world, the unreal or *Maya,* as the final truth. For those who do not at this point turn back to their false world picture, with its apparent but treacherous security, there lies a mighty vantage point in the experience of Emptiness.

Is it not dangerous to believe in the dictum "I am not the body," for would people not be inclined to neglect their body and consequently anything connected with the physical welfare of the people, as we have seen happening, for example, in India?

"I am not the body" has only value as a deeply felt truth; then it can open the door to a new dimension of being. As a belief or concept, accepted from hearsay, it has little significance and is likely to cause more confusion.

Now, who is saying that it is dangerous to accept this dictum? Is it not the mind that says so, and would one expect anything different from an entity that fears to be cast aside so radically? For "I am not the body" is only half a statement of truth; the other half is "I am not the mind either," since body and mind are inextricably interwoven and in reality are one. The mind, by virtue of its inherent nature, can never accede to its own depreciation.

Some may adduce the classical ideal of *mens sana in corpore sano* as being relevant here and as an argument for bodily perfection. Even granting that some correlation could exist between a healthy body and a "healthy" mind, the question is: What does one mean by a "healthy mind"? Is it a mind that has a high I.Q., that exhibits genius in a specialized skill, perhaps in some respects approaching the idiot savant, or is it an all-round mind that is reasonably clever overall, but not outstanding in any particular direction, perhaps in some ways approaching a mediocre mind? And by the same reasoning, but inversely, would someone who, by mere accident of birth, disease or mishap, is blessed with a little less than perfect physique, be written off as a no-hoper, physically, mentally, and spiritually? To even consider such spiritual elitism is, by its very absurdity, to reject it offhand. Were a perfect physical condition to be an essential requirement, practically no one would attain realization. What the world does not recognize is that no physically handicapped person is ipso facto spiritually handicapped. (We are not speaking about severe mental impairment, however.) Perhaps the reverse is rather the case: because of his different perspective on the grosser material level, his awareness might well be more sensitive to the deeper, non-material levels of his existence.

In sum, your question has been induced by the mistaken notion that body and mind can somehow be manipulated toward spiritual advantage; and that a healthy mind is the same thing as a liberated mind. Nothing could be farther from the truth. A "liberated mind" is really a contradiction in terms, for it is ignorance that empowers a mind, and as soon as ignorance is dispelled, the mind ceases to exist or, as Sri Ramana Maharshi put it, the mind drops into the Heart, which is the same as the Self. Others have referred to the ensuing state as one of "No-Mind," in which all idea of "doership" has come to an end and all action is automatic, spontaneous, and ever right; at the same time, all unproductive thoughts have ceased and thinking proceeds only where needed. Then what prevails is a state of Wholeness, which to me is the only true Health, in which body, mind and senses have been absorbed into the spirit.

What happens after death?

After death, you return to the state you were in before your so-called "birth." Actually, the term "return" is not quite accurate, since you are in that state all the time, regardless of time. It is only that the superstructure of body, mind and senses is absent. But even now, while body, mind and senses are present, their matrix is ever in evidence as the silent background, which is the very Ground of your being. Therefore, while the body-mind is still in place, utilize its presence to explore this whole question. Inevitably, the moment will arise when you fully know and then spontaneously discard the foreground, the entire scene in space-time, and thus abide in the eternal background as your true Self.

Is Life really worth living?

This is not a legitimate question in the first place, for there is no one who is living — that is just our basic delusion — there is only Living, Being. Or, as it has been put: "We are *being* lived," where when properly understood, it appears there is not even a "we." The individual is absolutely nonexistent; there is only something that resembles an individual but is, in effect, a kind of optical illusion in the mental realm.

Isn't the man who is about to commit suicide because of mental depression just like the man who is on the verge of Enlightenment?

No. Actually, both men represent antithetical cases. The man contemplating suicide is trying to kill that which does not even exist; he does not know yet that he is Nothingness itself. The man on the verge of enlightenment, realizing the Void, knows he is Nothing; he is already dead or about to die there and then. So in that case, where is the entity who is depressed, when there is only Nothingness looking at Nothingness? *Who* is depressed, when no one is there? Once Nisargadatta was confronted with a *sadhaka* who thought himself to be at that point, the threshold of realization, yet kept complaining about being depressed; Maharaj answered that he would have to go on doing much more meditation.

In my meditation, how can I go within, when I don't exactly know where is within and without?

I don't think a precise definition of "within" and "without" is a problem in meditation. "Without" is whatever the senses present and which for the most part is automatically projected outside the body; also the thoughts (desires, fears, hopes, expectations, etc.) that flow from these various sense perceptions. Going within is simply to reverse this process and *recede*; that is, follow back these mental processes to their various points of origination. It is as Nisargadatta has stated: Going back to one's rearmost level of perception and being; and Maharshi as: Turning the mind inward and tracing back all thought to the Heart (or real Self).

5

THINKING IS A DOUBLE-EDGED SWORD

I am somewhat confused in that there seems to be a contradiction between Krishnamurti's statement that thought can never lead one to liberation and Ramana Maharshi's words that thought can be used effectively to kill the mind.

Understood correctly, there is truth in both statements, paradoxically. Going along with thought and getting lost in its infinite ramifications and by-ways is like missing the forest for the trees. This is what we normally do, we flow along with the thought without being aware of our predicament: that thought is drawing us ever deeper into a quagmire. After all, thought can only lead to *more* thought; it will never lead us to the thought-free state, and in our state of agitation we are not even aware of the intervals between the thoughts. In this condition, our only respite is an occasional short interval of blissful, dreamless sleep. This is essentially what Krishnamurti points out, that the only tool we have at our disposal is awareness — the waking-up to the tyranny we have voluntarily submitted to. Choiceless awareness is the only way out, since choice means duality, preference, and so on, which is the very fuel that keeps the thought process going. Therefore, "choiceless" means that the awareness acts purely as mirror, thereby emasculating thought.

Ramana's admonition to investigate "Who Am I?" and to trace the "I"-thought back to its origin in the Heart is essentially the same recipe in slightly different words but on a deeper level — the level of *advaita* or non-duality, which embraces all that *is*, not just the mental level. Therefore, the prescription will be all the more effective and may lead to a transformation of one's total being, not merely one's psychological condition. The *sadhana* prescribed is to examine every thought and trace it back to its source. Rather than flowing with it and thereby giving the thought some legitimacy, one goes in the opposite direction. One looks at the thought with curiosity and love and finds out whence it has arisen. It is like following a river upstream and discovering its source in the mountain. This inquiry tends to have the effect of pushing back thought to its baseline; it puts the genie of corrupting mentation back into the bottle of pure non-differentiated awareness or "I-am-ness." For every thought contains a first thought, where "first" is not meant just in the chronological sense but denotes the primary supporting thought that gives energy, direction and vitality to all other thoughts and thought patterns embroidered on it.

For example, I have a certain thought and discover

that it has arisen because I find myself in a certain situation. The "I"-thought always arises from a certain situation, within a particular frame of reference; it cannot arise in a vacuum. If there isn't such an underlying situation, there is no thought — only a state of Beingness. And the same applies for action, and the motives for actions, for these are the thoughts and words enacted. Just find this out for yourself.

Ordinarily, I accept the situation — it is my only "given" but by having made it into a false Absolute, I miss the real Absolute. Thus, I either think along with the thought flowing from that situation or, at best, look at it in choiceless awareness. But now what if I go one step further? That is, I examine the "source situation" in the same way that I examine the thought flowing from it. With curiosity, with total attention — in short, with love. I may find that the situation that gave rise to the thought has itself arisen from another situation, a broader frame of reference. I will not be deterred by this and so spontaneously, automatically, my full attention flows to that earlier, more basic situation, and so on, to ever more fundamental situations until I arrive at a primordial point where there is literally nothing anymore; the central "I"-thought — through which I had invented or created my little "self" — is exposed and the whole thought structure collapses like a house of cards. In the words of Sri Ramana Maharshi, it collapses back into the Heart whence it originated.

All this will perhaps be clearer by giving a practical example. One has just suffered a serious loss, which the ordinary person would term "devastating." The total attention looks not only at what is lost but also, and more importantly, at who or what it is that has "suffered" the loss. The thought of "loss" leads me to the point in time and space when I first became associated with that which got lost. Obviously, the latter could be a physical possession, or a close and cherished association with another human being, a pet, with a group of people, or even with an idea that one is identified with and that has been demolished for one reason or another. Rolling back the thought, I see the situation when the association first came about and also my earlier condition before it had come about.

Another example is the feeling of "lack" caused by "desire" unfulfilled. There is nothing wrong with desire in itself, but when any desire gets to dominate our life in a chronic way, it becomes like a disease, an enslavement. So what needs to be done is to give full attention to the situation when the desire first sprang into life, and to clearly realize that it was not imposed from the outside but was voluntarily adopted in the first place, initially perhaps barely consciously through insidious societal conditioning and later as an ingrained habit or *vasana* and becoming part of our actual being. In all this, it is important to realize the power of thought; one actually *is* one's thoughts. The process of liberation begins therefore with the clear seeing of the initial situation in which the particular thought or desire took root.

In both these examples the feeling of "lack" will not have disappeared completely until I have possibly tra-

versed several earlier, more fundamental situations or frames of reference. Finally, I see that the very earliest situation did come about by considering myself as a "body" — that is, an "object" or physical entity existing in space and time. I then must pursue this line of examination further to the original state before having become associated with a body. I then revert, at least in my mind's eye, to the state of pure Presence, or the pure "I-am-ness" or Beingness, which is the background upon which all perception and thought appear.

Thus, at the very moment that I take away any "absoluteness," any legitimacy from any of "my" situations feeding the thought process, *there is no longer any situation* and no more thought at all. When all the frames of reference have been taken away, only Silence prevails. I have then discovered my original nature and I find myself in the perfect state in which there is no longer any lack, only "fullness" and bliss, and so no more motive for any action.

Thought has ended without any suppression on my part. I have used thought all right, but I have not been caught or enslaved by it. In fact, I have bypassed thought entirely by using the only weapon at my disposal, the attention, and have finally merged with the Awareness or Beingness that is my real nature. This is exactly the same process as inferred by Nisargadatta Maharaj's admonishment: Reverse, go back to the point before your birth. Birth is nothing more than the primordial source situation, the matrix, from which all thought, all images and all concepts spring. By reversing, one arrives at a pre-personality stage in which there is the freedom to use a personality wherever the situation warrants but no longer any identification with it. Thus, one is what *is*, before a "one" came into the picture. There is a stepping out of time and space and a feeling of total transparency which thought cannot touch.

Whereas the Krishnamurtian choiceless awareness may result in a momentary suspension, a temporary paralysis of the thought process, the *sadhana* prescribed by Ramana Maharshi penetrates to the primordial causes of thought, extending all the way to the *vasanas* — the deeply rooted tendencies and habits of seeing things and acting upon them in a fixed way — that must be dissolved before one can rest in pure Consciousness.

Generally speaking, the Oriental religions and philosophies seem to denigrate thinking. For example, in Hinduism, the highest stage that man can attain is believed to be that of the "thought-free" state. Why is that?

Thinking, usually considered in the West to be a higher function, is actually a purely mechanical process on all levels. Our thinking has essentially evolved from the most primitive reflexive action and forms one continuum with it in all grades of its development. It distinguishes itself from its incipient forms only by its complexity and refinement but has retained its purely deterministic character. (For these reasons, thought is considered by some to be a form of matter, which leaves open the question of what is matter and why we should have

to categorize everything.) Thinking is driven by the pleasure-pain principle, which in turn is the product of experience and memory.

The real "higher function" is actually the ability *to look* at thinking without being drawn into further "thinking." Thus, to be simply aware of the contents of consciousness, without adding to it, is of a different dimension than thought. Being from moment to moment, it is not deterministic and therefore is a "free-ing" vector in itself.

Why is thought neverending, when we all know that that is exactly where our problem lies?

I suspect this unwanted continuity is part of our survival mechanism. Thought is necessary for physical survival. If there were some controlling entity that could turn thought on and off like a spigot, who is to say that laziness would not prevail and leave thought unavailable most of the time, thereby lowering our state of readiness to fend for ourselves. Isn't that what is happening in certain states of *samadhi*, when we are helpless and unprotected? Even with this continuous thought process, nature has given us some extra assist with the biological "fight or flight" mechanism activated by the secretion of adrenaline, increasing our alacrity toward self-defense.

But, in a more serious vein, "I," being the controlling entity, so-called, is no other than thought, and does not really exist as such; that is, the "controller" is the "controlled," so there is no outside agency to regulate the process of thinking. Therefore, the answer to the question must be found in the nature of thought itself. You see, the Second Law of Thermodynamics, with its concept of entropy, applies also to thought, especially if thought is considered to be a form of matter, as some philosophers view it. In physics, "entropy" can be thought of "as a measure of how close a system is to equilibrium."[1] Physicists further state that all systems in nature appear to continually tend to maximize entropy. Thus, thought is continually churning to achieve lower tension; that is, toward psychological neutrality. In other words, it is always engaged in problem solving. Entropy seeks to steer things towards equilibrium, simplicity, uniformity, silence, peace. The process goes on almost uninterruptedly, day and night, whether we are conscious of it or not. Even in our sleep, dreams serve the process of filing the brain's contents, sorting things out, reducing the complex thought constructs to simpler ones, and eventually the latter to the perfect equilibrium of oblivion or maximum psychological entropy. So, paradoxically, on one level, thought is the greatest hindrance to liberation; on a deeper level, there is an ongoing process that works darkly in our favor towards the ultimate freedom and peace.

What is the purpose of life?

Whose purpose? Show me the "who" behind the "whose," and I will show you the purpose of life.

1 Funk & Wagnalls New Encyclopedia.

For years I have been obsessed with the question whether life has any meaning and have found none. Should I therefore live as though life is meaningless and forget about seeking for meaning?

The problem lies not with the apparent meaninglessness of life but with him who seeks for meaning in it. Why do we need meaning? And what could such meaning be? Another goal to pursue beyond this life, thereby devaluing the latter to a mere prelude? A comforting concept for some future happiness? Only an unhappy person will engage in such pursuits; a happy person is content with whatever *is.* To him the meaning of life is Living, Being. Bliss is when one has nothing to lose and nothing to gain — the thought-free state.

I have the impression that notwithstanding the ongoing crisis in consciousness that you have talked about and the fact that interest in New Age-type subjects, alternative forms of healing, shamanism, etc., has become noticeably stronger, interest in pure advaita *seems to be on the wane. Do you agree with this assessment and how do you explain it?*

You may well be right in this evaluation. Whether it concerns a minor or major trend is hard to judge at this stage, but by and large, I think that people are shying away from anything that might wake them up from their deep slumber. In other words, they tend to favor the status quo. What they are basically interested in is pseudo spirituality which does not require anything at all on their part but feeds their desire for more and more sensate values. This seems to be the societal trend all over the world; but in this case the trend is not our friend, as the saying goes. And although the torch of true *advaita* will ever be transmitted, at the moment this torch seems more like a little candlelight.

What we are seeing now is that all our activities are directed towards greater "individuation" or personal fulfillment, so-called; and people are not aware that all this "doing" leads only to cultivation of a false self or ego, taking us farther and farther away from simple Being, our natural state. This is probably what J. Krishnamurti, in one of his conversations with David Bohm, referred to when he stated that at some time in the past mankind took a wrong turn. Also, it may be relevant that in the Hindu scriptures our present age is described as the *Kali Yuga*, the final era of deterioration and degradation.

All this is speculation, however, but what is certain is that beneath it all the Universal law of entropy applies, on all levels, including the physical and the spiritual. Under this law, everything strives to return to its original state of rest; thus, the magically wound-up Universe of *Maya* ever tends to run down to its potential rest position, the state of maximum entropy. (I must, however, emphasize the word *tends*, because whether such an ultimate state of equilibrium is ever reached is beyond our ken.) Isn't it this tension that keeps all things going? What else is there? From the conventional point of view, this seems incomprehensible, even disorderly and ultimately meaningless; from a spiritual point of view and in accordance with the deepest intuition, it appears totally natural. It represents the eternal battle between "what appears to be," represented by *Maya*, and the real, the "what *is*," or the Absolute, and perhaps on a different plane, between Evil and Good.

The path of the spiritual aspirant is to give himself over to this supreme law of entropy, which means a willingness to die physically and/or psychologically. This means "letting go," both of the body when its time has come and of all the little goals and projects that the psyche is constantly concocting towards "self"-substantiation and "self"-justification. The "dying" is the movement towards the rest condition, which takes place physically as well as psychologically, and our pliability in this respect may more than any intellectual speculation or manipulation express our true understanding and fulfillment of the purpose or meaning of life.

I did not ask to be born into this miserable world. What do I do with my life? It all seems so utterly sterile and meaningless.

The meaning of your existence is primarily to realize your true nature, that you are not just an "individual," so that your life may stand in service of the world as a whole and make it a little less miserable. All else is mere entertainment, without ultimate meaning, as Nisargadatta put it so poignantly.

But once you have realized your true nature, when

individuality has been seen for the illusion it is and so has been transcended once and for all, there is only the Totality. Now where could the Totality go? It is at once everything, completely fulfilled — it is Fulfillment itself. Therefore, the question of meaning cannot apply for one, or more accurately for That, which has realized Itself. We can only talk of "meaning" when there still is intentionality, direction, a movement from here to there, from incomplete to complete, applying to a fragment, the false image of an "entity." It could not possibly apply to that which by definition is Everything, Complete and Perfect in Itself.

6

INQUIRY — MAN'S HIGHEST AND NOBLEST ACTIVITY

Is it possible for one to wake up to the spiritual life without a guru or having studied the ancient scriptures? In other words, how does a modern westerner come straight to the point without traversing all sorts of esoteric byways? How does such a person come to rediscover from his own experience the thousands of years' old wisdom of India known as advaita*?*

The question really is: Can one find out what it's all about, starting with nothing — no specialized knowledge of metaphysics or science, no indoctrination of any kind? My answer to this is yes; perhaps not for everybody, but in principle, yes, because then one starts off with a fresh mind, a beginner's mind — which is half the battle. But even then guidance — either inwardly or outwardly — is essential. Whether we realize it or not, Guru is always helping us along.

Most of us know too much, we are too educated, too clever by half when it comes to spirituality, and too set in our ways. All this interferes with the search into the unknown, since the known can never contact the "unknown," another dimension.

If you will permit me to quote from my own experience, in the late fifties my search had started in earnest, upon becoming acquainted with the teaching of J. Krishnamurti, Sri Ramana Maharshi, and various Zen Masters. They represented Guru to me, and led me to *vichara* (Inquiry). Yet, my exploration into what *is* proceeded along independent lines, as a logical extension of my scientific upbringing and my own inherent curiosity. My initial inquiry concerned the underlying nature of superficial appearances and phenomena, the reality lying behind sensory observation. More specifically, I was interested to probe the meaning of the evidence provided by the sense organs, which is the raw material for the mind's functioning. My investigation proceeded somewhat on the following lines.

First and foremost, the mind perceives in its field of observation a multitude of separate forms, entities distinct in space and time. Thought, for the purpose of recognition, then attaches names to these regularly recurring forms and sensory experiences, which is the language. The common perception prevails that language discloses something about the real nature of the objects and concepts defined. However, I soon realized with something of a shock that it does nothing of the sort; it merely makes communication possible by enabling us to refer to the same things, an aspect that I have discussed more fully in my book *Crisis in Consciousness*.

It also dawned upon me that the boundaries of these discrete entities were determined by the makeup of the sense organs and their various mediums of operation and were not an exclusive property of the objects themselves. Take, for example, the sense of vision. The boundaries of objects are determined by the reflection on their external surfaces of radiation within a certain range of the electromagnetic wave spectrum, that which we call "visible light." The various shapes perceived in this fashion are therefore not independent from the medium and organs of observation. This means they have a dependent existence and so have no absolute reality. They exist only insofar as "I" exist.

The parameters of my own "I-ness" are equally relative or arbitrary. For example, were my sense organs of a different constitution, the body might be delineated by its heat radiation or by another section of the electromagnetic wave spectrum. In that case, my physical "form" would be utterly different. To ask which one is the correct or the "more correct" form of the "me" is to see at once its nebulous nature from a reality point of view, and more specifically, that the question is closely intertwined with the nature of the observer who tries to define the object. I have thus arrived ineluctably at the conclusion and insight of unicity: the subject and object are part of one continuum, one process, and it becomes therefore quite meaningless to talk of the nature of the object as a "given" or absolute (as Kant did when talking about the "thing in itself") without considering the subject. And also vice versa: it further follows that the nature of the "subject," within this subject-object relationship, is not as clear-cut as we had assumed. Even physically "I" am not what I thought I was, and furthermore, what passes for one's self, psychologically — that is, the "personality" or "individuality" — are certain accretions, the qualities that the mind has arbitrarily identified with the physical form. Thus, we can see that each actually creates his own reality!

The evidence of my senses is also in another way — qualitatively — quite misleading. Although we talk of sense perception as direct evidence, it is always a product of inference. For instance, my tactile sense tells me that a steel rod is quite solid, as against mud or clay which exhibit different degrees of "softness." This is my experiential impression on the macromolecular level. But when I descend to a more fundamental level — the molecular or atomic level — I find that most of this apparent solidity is actually empty space. Once again, my impression on the everyday level of experience has prima facie proved to be a lie. What is perceived as "object" is ever only in relation to a subject. No object as such exists; it is always only an impression! In this way, without having any scriptural knowledge, nor knowledge of quantum mechanics, but merely by observation, reflection and common sense, I have stumbled upon the age-old concept of *Maya!* And by the same means, I have also started to partake of that most essential of acquisitions: Self-knowledge or the genuine spiritual knowledge.

All that I can know of the manifested world is what appears to be, what my sense organs and mind create for the "me," which is now seen to be the Absolute Subject or Subjectivity itself. In actuality, neither subjects nor objects exist; there is only unicity or *advaita*: non-duality, upon which all the dualities are projected. Ordinary knowledge is always *Maya*; we may call it "false" but it is really a projection of the mind. Thus, it is seen that in a sense, when properly understood, even *Maya* is real, because whatever can be known within a subject-object relationship is ever only that which makes its appearance in consciousness. And since there is no consciousness apart from its contents — consciousness *is* its contents — *Maya* is consciousness. This is what the deepest spiritual thinkers have always taught.

Once you have the understanding of your real nature, let it pervade the whole of your being. Stabilize in it by consciously acting from it in all your relationships until all traces of the false, conceptual persona have been dissolved in reality.

Can you tell me whether the world is real or unreal, if there is an answer to that question?

There is an answer, but for that you must look toward the one who is asking the question. As always, and paradoxically, the question arises from the answer, is already established in the answer. You see, you are the answer. If you consider yourself as an enduring entity, separate from the world, then to you the world is real. But if you understand your real nature, you will see that the world is a creation of yourself, evanescent as a dream. It manifests itself only so long as there is a dreamer; but it has no independent existence and therefore is unreal.

In a certain sense, it can be said that the world is both real and unreal. It is real *to you*, in an exclusive relationship; at the same time, without that particular qualifier, it is an unwarranted extrapolation to state that the world is real. Remember, to a person born deaf, the world is silent and to one born blind the world is dark. Such statements about the world remain relativist, without the least absolutist significance, so long as the "you," as perceiver, remains an unknown factor. It immediately shifts the inquiry toward the nature of that "you." It is analogous to an inquiry into fear, where to properly understand and overcome it, one must ask: Who has the fear? There is fear only so long as there is a "me" that incorporates the fear. The moment it is realized that the "me" is a concoction from and by memory, the fear is dissolved. Just so, the world appears real only so long as one lives from one's own imagined identity: identification with an arbitrary personality-image largely accepted through feedback from hearsay. Thus, to one in which the global apperception prevails and the personal element as perceiver has disappeared, the world is unreal and no longer acknowledged.

Is a guru necessary for showing us the way?

First, who or what is "guru"? If one can become clear about the real meaning of that term, the answer to the question will appear quite naturally. The primary fact is that everyone needs help to be put onto the right path, and this can only be fully appreciated when the true nature of that which needs help dawns upon us. In other words, to fully appreciate the question of guru a modicum of self-knowledge is required.

The guru can manifest in different forms, but as already stated, he is always essential. Without guru, absolutely nothing could be done. This will become understood when one goes into the nature of the individual aspiring to liberation. That so-called "individual" is an artifact, has no actual existence except as a self-perpetuating mechanical entity. Once set into motion, it will continue to spin out its imaginary existence ad infinitum, due to its own inertia. Therefore, anything it strives for will still be part of its own dream world; the unreal can never approach the real, it can only disappear. This is the real reason why help is needed. And quite logically, this help is applied in the only way possible, by shocking the unreal to realize and give up its own falsehood by challenging all its assumptions and thereby confronting it with reality. Then automatically, the unreal self collapses and what is left only is the real. In other words, the entire mechanical process must disappear. Since this normally does not occur by itself, as any efforts by the process to escape from itself can only be extensions of itself, help is needed and that principle which helps we call "guru."

This guru can take the form of an external master or it may be one who is no longer in the body. You may have heard that saying: "The real guru is within." So even if you meet an external guru, he functions only as the reflection, the external manifestation, of that one true inner guru, who is the same guru for all beings. To the guru, there is neither space nor time, because he is the life principle in everyone that transcends the body-mind entity. You see, the real guru is always present, because guru is the only thing that is ever present as the real. My individual being covers over that reality, but guru is nothing but the reality itself. He is your very Self. That is why he is always there for us, ever waiting to give us a push in the right direction by waking us from the dream and so dissolving that false individuality. For this reason they say in India: "Worship the guru as the highest god," because without guru you are nothing — just a bundle of mechanical, instinctual reflexes — and nothing can ever be done, darkness will prevail. The very word "guru" tells us a story; it is a composite of "gu," which means "darkness," and "ru" meaning "dispeller." Hence, the true function of guru is as dispeller of darkness. And when darkness is dispelled, there remains only the light and that is universal.

For a long time I have been puzzled by the question: Why is there a world — whether you consider it as Maya *or reality, that is not my point here — but why is there anything at all? Why are we faced with Existence? By whose request has the world scene been summoned? And why should there not just be "nothing"?*

You may not realize it, but this is one of those questions

that for very good reasons is "verboten." You are not permitted to ask this question, for it leads to all kinds of logical absurdities.

The possibility that there may be nothing at all could only have been raised by one who is divorced (alienated) from his real Self, by a brain that is functioning purely in computer mode — yes-no, one-zero, etc. — that is, dualistically. To the one who has clearly seen that he is the Totality and that there can be no such thing as "nothingness" (in the nihilistic sense), it must logically follow that there can be no such thing as Death (in the usual sense, as the opposite of Life); and if there is Death, it is only an empirical designation of a particular mode of functioning, or perhaps more accurately, of "non-functioning" within Consciousness and therefore still subsumed under the category of Life. Life and Death, commonly viewed as a pair of opposites, is clearly seen to be an illusion!

At this point, someone may come up with the objection that he does not feel he is the Totality, because he clearly perceives a multitude of separate creatures and entities, appearing and disappearing ("dying"), which clearly contradicts my previous conclusion. To this person, I would like to say two things. First, I would ask, to whom do these separate creatures appear? The answer must be: To "you," as an individual, whose particular identity as a "person," separate and independent from others, is in question. In other words, it is a cyclic argument! The truthfulness of my observation is only so strong as the established truth about the observer. So long as I do not know my self, any conclusion about the perceptions by that self have no validity.

Second, when the person says: I perceive so many separate creatures, what does he really see? He sees a multitude of forms, of bodies, and from this he jumps to the conclusion that he sees so many selves. But for this, he must necessarily have identified the bodies with individualities, with separate "selves," which he has done because he mistakenly identified his own "self" with a body in the first place! We are maintaining the very opposite: that there is one indwelling principle, which we choose to call "Self," which inhabits a multitude of physical forms. Moreover, since these forms appear and disappear in consciousness, they must have their existence in consciousness and be of the nature of consciousness itself, just like waves in water are still water only. Waves may appear in and on water, but they have no existence in themselves, apart from the water. Just so the apparent individual forms have no existence apart from the consciousness, which is the underlying and indwelling principle.

One should further consider (meditate upon) the following points:

(1) You, who are asking, are also part of this world scene. So you are asking in effect: Why should I not be absent, or not be here? Only someone other than yourself can ask this question. For this, you should know that "self" thoroughly.

(2) You cannot wind up (terminate) the world, even mentally, for in doing so, you are actually maintaining

the world; your action at that point is an action by the world, for you are part of this world! Do you see the double-bind situation?

Another way to see this is to state that for you a state of Nothingness is the Unknown; it is totally beyond one's experience, for as long as one exists there is experience (of something). Therefore, "nothing" is beyond our ken; it is simply the projection by the mind of the opposite of "something."

(3) Concepts of Existence and Nonexistence are both made possible only by thought; as a pair of opposites they are mental categories and therefore belong to the realm of *Maya*, the unreal. These opposites can only occur to the thought machine. But that which makes possible their conception within thought, and even the very thinking itself, is of a different dimension. It is the "*is*-ness," the real, the source of *Maya*, Creation itself, timeless and beyond both existence and nonexistence, beyond any possibility of visualization by the mind. The truth of this can only be intuited through transcendence of the mind, when all thought and speculation on this point cease and the mind has become extraordinarily quiet.

Is there any measure by which to gauge one's progress, spiritually speaking?

Yes, there is such a yardstick but it is not a very popular one for it entails a good deal of pain. What is involved is a certain degree of visualization: to keep in mind the things that you hold dearest in your life —

your material, mental and cultural possessions, your human capabilities, your dearest relationships, and ultimately your very means of cognizing and functioning in the world, your body-mind — and contemplate what it would feel like if you lost all that. In other words, in every situation in life contemplate a worst-case scenario. If you can do that with equanimity, you are an advanced soul, perhaps even liberated. If not, you need to continue with your meditation.

Why should I contemplate a worst-case scenario when I am a born optimist? You may be a pessimist, but I am not and so all this does not apply to me.

To tell the truth, I am not a pessimist either, but neither am I an optimist or even a so-called "realist." These three categories of persons, in essence, amount to the same thing, they are "unrealists," for they deal with unreality only. They say the worst suffering is when bad things happen to nice people. I say suffering is when things, both "good" and "bad," happen to "nice" and "not so nice" people, in other words when things happen to *persons* or *individuals*. Now all that is unreality, from a spiritual point of view. You see, if you truly live in and with reality, which is the totality, how could things happen and *to whom* are they happening? Nothing can happen to you because you are everything, *and nothing ever happens to the whole*. Even on the level of logic that must be so: If something happened to the whole, then that would necessitate there being something besides the whole, right? And in that latter case, the "whole" would be incomplete, and so it could not be the whole. The pragmatic entity that functions as an "individual" has come about through the subdivision of the whole by thought and its identification with one of the fragments.

Thus, so long as you maintain this attitude of ever looking forward and backward, for things to happen and things that have happened, you keep intact the fragment to which things continue to be happening, both "good" and "bad." The "individual" exists only because things are happening; when things cease to happen, there is no longer an individual. Upon the disappearance of the "individual," the threatening cloud of things that may happen to "you" will have dissolved and you will be beyond this movement of time, the movement of desire and fear. In the resulting clear sky, the sun of what *is* shines timelessly in all its glory. That sun is your very Self.

Could you summarize for us in as few words as possible what needs to and can be done in a practical way to dispel the fundamental Ignorance most of us live with? I would like to take home something simple that I can remember and work upon so that I may come to some understanding.

The first step is to see one's own nothingness, non self-identity, etc., and thereby have an experience of the Emptiness. That is, I am not the body, mind or senses, nor the many concepts and images which they have called forth but, in first instance, I am consciousness, the sense of being present or Presence itself. This awareness is prior to everything: prior to body, prior to world, etc.

Second, being the consciousness, and also comprising the totality of space and time, and even transcending both, I am by extension and more profoundly and fundamentally the source of this consciousness. Having understood the nature of consciousness, it follows that I, as subject, am not merely that consciousness. Ultimately, the consciousness stands in relation to me as an object to a subject. Thus, upon "death" so-called, I am still That, which equals the state that I appeared to be before my "birth" so-called.

Nisargadatta Maharaj stresses courage as well as understanding as necessary ingredients in the quest. This ties in with his statement that the greatest difficulty after proper understanding has been attained is to emulate the teaching, to really let go of everything and actually "live" the teaching. For this courage is necessary as well as wisdom.

For about ten years I have been religiously practicing the path of bhakti, *which for my particular disposition, and in view of my Indian background, I feel is more suitable than the path of* jnana, *that you advocate. Also, I have a feeling that* bhakti *eventually leads to quite a different place than where* jnana *leads to. Notwithstanding my regular practice, my progress has been disappointingly slow, and I wonder where I could have gone wrong.*

The problem with your lack or absence of "progress" is exactly your belief in progress! You see, in the Real there is no progress. If there is progress, then you are not talking about the Real. Progress entails going from here to there, but in the Real you are where you are, once and for all — then you can say only "I am." There cannot be progress for the simple reason that you are away from time and space, which lead to the illusion called "progress."

Nothing good or bad can happen to you; you are in a condition which is Good, without possibility of amelioration or deterioration — that is, this "Good" does not allow for "better" or "worse." When something that is conventionally (or perhaps, better, "consensually") considered to be "good" appears to happen to "you," then it really happens to somebody or something other than yourself; similarly, when something considered "bad" happens to you, then it actually happens to someone other than yourself, do you understand that? They happen to an entity that you are mistakenly referring to as "myself," that person who is on a path of *bhakti* or *jnana*. Even though you are on one of those paths, and I am certainly not discouraging you from being there, please never consider your real "You" to be located there or have anything to do with it. The state of the Real knows no coming and going whatsoever. One has arrived, but also one has never departed! Do you understand the subtlety and beauty of all that?

Among the several paths that may lead to spiritual emancipation — jnana *or knowledge,* bhakti *or devotion, and karma yoga or selfless action, which approach do you consider most suitable for the westerner?*

It has nothing to do with being a westerner or easterner, it has to do with your individuality, your inclinations or *vasanas*, which approach is most suitable to you. I would say only, if your favored path is devotional, then stick to your guru once you have found one that you trust and follow his instructions implicitly, which really means surrender to him. When following the path of inquiry, you must also follow your guru's teachings faithfully but, in addition, it is most helpful to take note of what other teachers have said. That is, it is most important to come to grips with the teaching above and beyond the utterings of different sages, but as their common denominator as it were. Finally, and most importantly, one's understanding should be honed and tested within one's own consciousness in everyday living. For most of us this is a lifelong activity. At the very end, all the different paths to liberation merge into one.

I read that by means of biofeedback one can produce the alpha *brain waves, which occur in altered states of consciousness, and especially in the liberated state. Do you advocate experimentation with biofeedback to facilitate spiritual emancipation?*

Biofeedback is a physical process and may have usefulness on that level, the body-mind level. *Alpha* waves may well be a by-product on the level of physicality of a change in consciousness. However, it would be a mistake to think that mere manipulation of the electrical condition of the brain will lead to the egoless state. The ocean gives rise to the waves on its surface, but this does not mean that the latter can bring the ocean into being.

To describe various mental states, you are using the term "altered states of consciousness," a term which has come into vogue recently but is actually totally inappropriate. Since everything is Consciousness, and there is nothing beside it, logically, Consciousness cannot be a state of something else; it must be a non-state. There can be no derivatives of Consciousness; the various mental states which we experience and to which we ascribe some independent reality are only superimpositions on the Consciousness, like clouds appearing on a clear sky. Another aspect of Consciousness is Bliss. The mind being forever moving, giving rise to all the various moods and emotions, obscures this bliss aspect of the Consciousness. But at times, when the mind relaxes, for example, when enjoying Nature or listening to beautiful music, we become filled with this joy, which we then ascribe to the scenery or the music. But in actual fact, we are getting a taste of the universal bliss which is our very Self.

Immediately upon waking from deep sleep, there is this blissful state of pure attention or non-duality without any awareness of the limited self, with as yet no identifications. How can this bliss go on when we are called upon to function dualistically in society?

Only when we are seeing the various roles we assume as purely that, *assumed* roles. Then we play those roles that are expected from us, more from consideration for the other unreal "individualities" than anything else. For others can only recognize and relate to us on that level, that is, insofar as we enact our various assigned roles. The self-realized, however, remains ever aloof as the witness of the various parts as well as the Totality in which everything is being enacted. He watches the actors as well as the background against which the play takes place, without ever any identification with the witnessed taking place. In this way, the bliss of being purely the Self is ever in attendance.

From what I have read in one of your books, you seem to equate choiceless awareness with "I am That," and I have some difficulty with the identification implied in the latter expression. I do not really understand how the one leads to the other. Could you elucidate this?

Let me try to clarify this matter of choiceless awareness first. One becomes acutely aware that there are no absolute values; that whatever one appears to be is nothing but concept, conditioning. Hence, there is no point in judging, approving or disapproving, approximating oneself to an ideal, or clinging to anything at all; one perceives everything with full acceptance, choicelessly, for there is no longer any process of comparison with fixed standards of what "ought to be." The mind has fallen silent in total letting-go. One pursuing this to the very end realizes his Emptiness or Nothingness. That one *is*, and everything else is a superimposition by the unreal, or *Maya*.

Regarding the expression "I am That," there is no question of anyone identifying himself with "That." It is just not possible: One can identify only with something that is known. In fact, "That" denotes what remains when all that one knows has been transcended. So one who has eliminated everything in choiceless awareness will understand or feel that he is the Emptiness, the Nothingness, and can truly say "I am That." Then it may be clear that That cannot be known, because it is not an entity or a concept; therefore, it is not possible to be understood by the mind like a subject understands an object. One can only *be* That; in fact, nothing but That exists. So, after correcting one's mistaken identity, one sees oneself as the Totality, as That only. Thus, through the negation of what one is not, one arrives at the positive of what one is. Realize this thing only, stabilize in this understanding and henceforth, live from that realization in all your thinking and actions.

7

Two Maverick Masters — J. Krishnamurti and Nisargadatta

Many people talk about J. Krishnamurti and Indian advaitic *sages such as Ramana Maharshi and Nisargadatta Maharaj in the same breath, as you also seem to have done in the past, but more recently, I get the impression that you have distanced yourself somewhat from Krishnamurti. How do you really see K's teachings in relation to that of the great Indian sages? To me, they seem practically identical.*

In my early days, I was very much enamored by K's teaching and I still think it is valid; only it is not *advaita*. I believe that K will be enormously helpful but especially so for the beginner on the spiritual path. What he says is valid, but not the whole truth. It certainly is not *advaita,* in the purest sense of the word. Let me just mention very briefly those main aspects where I think he differs totally from *advaita*; then you can go into the various ramifications for yourself.

In K's teaching, there is nothing that is unchanging.

Everything is constantly changing, in a flux, and there is no eternal rest state, such as the *satchitananda* (existence-consciousness-bliss) of Hinduism. Second, in the psychological realm K admits non-duality, but he maintains an absolute division between the physical and the psychological worlds, as our scientists and philosophers in the main still do. Thus, he does not hold to the idea that even physically the separation between one individual and another is illusory. And third, K does not accept the idea of *Maya*, the vision that the entire manifest world is illusory, an appearance, superimposed on the unicity of the real. There you have it in a nutshell, the most basic differences between K and the Indian masters of *advaita*. On a less fundamental level, one might further mention the downgrading of the role of the guru in K's world-view. K advises never to listen to a guru, but it may be argued that he himself acted like a guru his entire life. In the beginning, I took K's word as gospel truth in this respect; now I know better and realize that with perhaps very few exceptions, people do not come to the essential truths by themselves. They need to have their eyes opened by a teacher. Although the real guru is ever within, almost everyone needs contact with an external guru, or literally, "dispeller of darkness."

In balance, it might be said on the positive side that Krishnamurti has introduced a whiff of spirituality into an otherwise indifferent and unknowing western world; and, negatively, that through the extreme stance adopted, he might have thrown out the baby with the bathwater, in cutting off his audience from the entire tradition of

Indian spirituality and the mystical tradition that runs through all the world's religions — the wisdom that Aldous Huxley referred to by the term *The Perennial Philosophy* in his book by that title.

Having said all that, I am not stating that a break-through to self-realization through K's teaching is impossible. In practical terms, to become established in non-duality, psychologically, may amount to or lead to the same thing as realization attained the classical way, through *bhakti* or *jnana*, especially since it concerns a state of being rather than one of knowing. But I feel it will be all that more difficult, if a whole area of our existence — the physical or material level — is left out of consideration. Indeed, K himself has stated on more than one occasion that nobody really understood his teaching.

I would like to ask you a number of questions regarding Sri Nisargadatta Maharaj's teaching, especially as it reaches us through the book The Nectar of Immortality. *I find that Maharaj sounds somewhat intolerant of visitors. For example, I read on page 72 of this book: "I am going to send you out of here." Why is he exhibiting such impatience, or am I misreading the passage?*

Maharaj often jostles his visitors. Some of these people came for reasons other than acquiring knowledge, for example, to score in a verbal skirmish. Maharaj saw through such persons quickly; besides, space in his abode was at a premium and he felt that everyone should have a chance to attend the dialogue sessions.

Maharaj seems to disregard body-mind phenomena. But the reality is "I am" and that I possess a body. Why reject it? Why not play along with the Maya?

You misread Maharaj here. He does not reject body-mind and its phenomena, only one's identification with it. Thus it is valid to say "I possess a body," but it is not valid to say "I am that body." As to your question, "Why not play along with the *Maya*?", that is exactly what Maharaj suggests: to go along with it, because one has understood its unreality. The error that almost everyone makes is to take it seriously and get involved with it.

Why do you think Maharaj states (in I Am That) *that the killer is hurt more than the killed?*

The killer departs from the point of view of his separate existence. His action is based entirely on that and therefore sets him back further from the essential revelation of unicity at which all living beings must eventually arrive. The killed, on the other hand, is not hurt at all; only his body is affected.

In Nectar of Immortality *(page 131), Maharaj says that "of all the species, the most evolved is the human being." What is it that evolves — the five basic elements or is it the mind flow?*

The human species is the most evolved in the sense that

it possesses the greatest potential to be conscious of itself, to know itself and to transcend its time-bound state. Of course, all this has come about through the play of the five elements and the three *gunas*. The five elements themselves do not evolve; they are primary, gross elements, but through their endless combinations and permutations with the *gunas*, different kinds of food bodies "evolve." As Maharaj would say, the quintessences of the food bodies give rise to creatures with varying levels of consciousness, whereas the indwelling principle is unvarying, having neither color nor design.

Now what is it that evolves? Only the body form — that is, bodily parameters such as posture, central nervous system, cortex, etc. As I said, the indwelling principle remains the same, but expresses itself differently, according to body form and design. (Think of a motor car: the engine and car body change, constantly evolve; the automobile principle, however, remains the same.)

The mind flow evolves insofar as the somatic changes can lead to more comprehensive states of consciousness. It is like opening up a window further on what *is*. But we must not give the connotation of "higher" to evolution here, because the thoughts forming the mind flow remain reactions to the impressions from the outside and dependent on the constitution of the sensory mechanism. The mind flow is restricted to be a purely mechanical process dependent on impressions (*samskaras*).

Since Beingness is the outcome of food, then if one varies the type of food eaten, can one affect one's state of consciousness or level of Knowingness?

The answer is "yes." It has long been a tenet in Hinduism that the type of food one consumes influences one's consciousness. Hence, they talk about *sattvic* food, *rajasic* food, etc. Generally, a *sattvic* diet is held to be most beneficial — that is, vegetarian and bland foods, no onions, no spices, etc. Maharaj himself did not restrict himself to such foods — he was not even a vegetarian. Obviously, he did not consider such a diet as mandatory for one's spiritual development.

Maharaj states in The Nectar of Immortality *(p. 95): "But the witness of the Consciousness is the highest principle — the Absolute." Does this imply that there could be information received from the Absolute, filtering down through universal consciousness to the body-mind? If so, is this what is referred to as "channeling," so popular today in New Age circles?*

Wishful thinking! No. The most refined manifestation of the Absolute is "witnessing." The Absolute itself, not having any attributes, is prior to consciousness and therefore prior to knowledge or information. Channeling and all such processes are part of the *Maya.*

On page 5 of the same book (Nectar of Immortality), *the* parabrahman *is referred to as that which prevails up to the eighth day prior to conception. Would you please tell me what defines the other seven days prior to conception? Maharaj in his conversations twice refers to a period of eight days.*

The "eight days" is merely shorthand for any period prior to conception. Elsewhere, Maharaj talks about a month, and so on. There is no particular significance to his use of the number eight. In fact, the Absolute prevails even now, regardless of time; only we are lost to it and distracted by such apparently fundamental events as "conception," "birth," and "death."

In Seeds of Consciousness, *conflicting statements appear about reincarnation being and not being a fact. This leaves me confused. How do you see this?*

On the face of it, Maharaj indeed makes contradictory statements about reincarnation, among other things. I can easily explain that. You see, the books are records of private discussions with individuals having different backgrounds and degrees of comprehension. They were not primarily intended to be published in book form for the general public. So, with beginners, Maharaj goes along with their various simple beliefs, including reincarnation. To more advanced students, Maharaj is ruthlessly outspoken. Furthermore, this problem of reincarnation is actually a secondary issue. If one understands the teaching as a whole, and particularly has gone into the question "Who Am I?," then reincarnation no longer appears to have any relevance; one sees through the matter and that is the end of it. For this reason, Maharaj, in the final stage of his life, was increasingly reluctant to even discuss this issue. The same, apparently ambivalent attitude one finds in Sri Ramana Maharshi's teachings and for identical reasons.

I think Maharaj is saying that one experiences the Absolute while the Beingness is between the sleep and waking states. The brain wave pattern is then between beta *and* theta, *presumably the* alpha *state. If one induces an* alpha *brain wave pattern, can one then experience the Absolute and be conscious of it?*

Maharaj's reference to "experiencing the Absolute" is not and cannot be that of the usual dualistic experience requiring a subject and object. Therefore, "experiencing" here means *being* the Absolute. Now, one ever is the Absolute, but one has not woken up to that fact. In the transition from waking to the sleep state, at the instant that the "I-am-ness" subsides, in that timeless moment, Maharaj maintains, it is possible to know one is purely the Absolute. At that point, the *Maya* state drops away and one enters another state — although Maharaj sometimes call this a "non-state."

As to "experiencing the Absolute" through inducing an *alpha* brain wave pattern, it may well be that the latter ever accompanies the former as its physiological counterpart, but it would be faulty logic to conclude that induction of *alpha* waves is all that is necessary to cause the experience of the Absolute. And even if it were possible to induce the experience in this manner, the resulting state would seem to me an inherently contradictory and so unstable mode. What or who is the inducing agent? The ego or mind, of course. So that which results can only be an unstable condition. Better to empty the mind, dispel all illusion, and simply be what remains: that Emptiness which one may call the Absolute.

I also have a question about something in Maharaj's teaching that I did not understand fully and hope you can clarify for me. It is his statement: "What you do not understand is matter."

Maharaj does not elucidate this fully, so I can only give you my point of view, which may or may not coincide with Maharaj's. We live in a mental Universe, and we ourselves are of the substance of mind or consciousness, yet we talk about "matter" as belonging to a separate mental realm. What do we designate as "matter"? All that which is experienced in a certain way by the sense organs, such as when we say that matter is tangible, has "solidity," "mass," exhibits inertia, etc. We think that science can explain what matter is. But science merely pushes back the frontiers of our ignorance. For what is "explanation" other than displacing the problem, restating it in different terms? Thus, in this particular case, we substitute various unknowns, concepts — a whole array of "fundamental particles," photons, wavicles, etc. — for what on the macro level is experienced as "matter." Please do not think that I allege these "particles" do not exist — they indeed have experiential validity and so are scientifically justified — but I am only saying that ontologically they are not an explanation of what matter is.

A further interesting point is that the various attributes of "matter" on the sensory or macro level are no longer valid or apparent on the sub micro and fundamental levels. Attributes such as hardness or softness, color, smell, taste, shape, and possibly even size and mass do not seem to matter anymore on a deeper level of reality. It appears then that we have profoundly misunderstood "matter," and that in actual fact there is no matter at all as a separate realm of experience. Ultimately, all experiences are appearances and disappearances in consciousness and therefore themselves also of the nature of consciousness. Delusion sets in the moment we regard these sensory impressions as anything more than just that and magically imbue them with some absolute reality.

Much of what Maharaj has said about matter can also be stated about "mind," which in our conventional thinking is regarded as something that has definite limits, is an entity of its own. Only because it is not understood for what it is, pure consciousness, does there appear to be a recognizable structure within that consciousness, to which we have assigned identity and various other characteristics. When "the mind" is fully understood, it is not just there anymore; it has become totally transparent. Thus, both matter and mind have been the subject of the same basic misunderstanding that is responsible for their division into separate realms. It must never be forgotten that they are mutually dependent concepts, since one can only be defined in terms of the other. Matter stands out as a separate reality just because mind exists; and mind stands out as a separate reality only because we have created the category of matter. So wipe away all concepts if you really want to understand. Then, in truth, there is only Consciousness, the substratum of all divisions and classifications. Just be mindful of that always, and you won't go far wrong in your study of spirituality.

What is really meant by the "I am," which is mentioned in certain spiritual writings and especially in the teachings of Sri Nisargadatta Maharaj?

"I am" is the essence of your manifestation and is also the essential part of your functioning, your being. It is the one indisputable statement that one can make about oneself without fear of contradiction. As soon as you add anything to that statement and qualify it, such as: "I am male or female, spiritual or worldly, rich or poor," you are on thin ice, since all these attributes can be argued or contradicted, or because they refer only to the bodily part of you and therefore beg the question as to your real being. So only "I am" is irrefutable. Without that "I am," the question could not have arisen in the first place; therefore the very question proves the truth of that "I am."

As I also stated, "I am" is the essential part of "you," of your functioning, since it is your sentience, your sense of being present, not however the sense of *you* being present — there is a huge difference. You see, the "you" comes into being only through the various attributes that one has gathered around that "I am" and that lend you your "identity." Without the living core of that "I am," however, you are only a corpse — a condition in which you would not know of yourself nor would anyone know that you are.

Finally, what we can say about this "I am" is that, since it is bereft of identity, it is literally unique, it is not restrained by space-time although it manifests through different bodies and at different points in time; there is not your "I am" and my "I am," there is only "I am" without emphasis on the personal pronoun. If I may for one moment bring up the well-known analogy of the movie projector, then the film is a particular "life" story, the projector is a particular body-mind entity, and the "I am" is the light which shines through a multitude of projectors and is not unique to any of them. And only that light, being unchanging, is real.

"I am" is realized through the transcendence of one's mistaken sense of identity, the idea that there is an "I am" as distinct from a "you are."

I have read your book The Wisdom of Sri Nisargadatta Maharaj *and I agree with your statement in the introduction that we must "see ourselves as the infinite expanse of consciousness which embraces all and everything." This is the heart of wisdom, I agree. I do not agree, however, that the approach to this consciousness can "never occur through direct conscious effort, by thought, by imagination." I most strongly take exception to this assertion. For me, it resembles too much the dogmatic non-dualism of Krishnamurti, which creates as its spokesmen short-tempered and irritable old men, intolerant of all but a rigid by-the-book* advaita. *I feel rather cramped and hindered in their presence, like a child who should be seen and not heard when grumpy old grandpa is in the room!*

The via negativa *method is to my understanding but a partial teaching, Robert. I find that there is a* via positiva, *an affirmative approach, which does not negate the negating mode that you propound. Thought, though it becomes tangled in illusions, though it may try to project its own limits upon the limitless, can also lead us to the threshold of the Real. To overcome the misuse, the illusion-creating propensity of thought, let us not spurn mind but let a directed mind merge in the light of Spiritual Mind.*

Though it is true that the reality of being is not contained in thought or imagination, it is also true that the right use of thought and imagination are part of the preparation. Your own books are an example of this, for each represents a concerted effort of thought — without which you would have had nothing to offer. Though it is true that "the finite can never embrace the infinite," it is also true that the infinite may embrace the finite and remain itself unbounded.

Robert, though Nisargadatta brilliantly expounds the non-dualist outlook, I find little compassion or tolerance in him. A great many spiritually sincere people still need the distinction between concepts of "personal self" and "universal self." It is a necessary transition period in a life. It may be the "learner's stage" as this teacher and Krishnamurti convey, yet I think it unwise to reject its training as lesser or unworthy. It would seem to promote a "spiritual egghead elite" of a type resembling the corps of aloof scientists who spurn the untrained thinking of us common laymen. To my mind, it leaves this troubled world destitute of the help we could provide it. It can shut off the heart from everyday experiences of love and beauty, leaving us mere observing intellects. Our reasoning leaves us unmoved in the face of suffering, for we readily divorce ourselves from identification with those who suffer. We become so detached as to be useless to others as real helpers or healers of the human condition. Robert, this is a path I do not wish to live. Though it may not be your intention, I think the misunderstanding of many can lead to this condition.

Before talking about taking conscious action, you should find out if the presumed "doer" of all that action exists in actuality. Because if he does not exist, you are pushing against the wind, as it were. You have created a self-image and assign certain actions to it. Actions do take place, but by whom? Who is the instigator? The mistake in perception originates with the creation of an arbitrary image, the self-image, which in turn has come about on account of faulty identification by thought with the body. The fact of the matter is that actions happen to "you," you do not produce the actions.

Hopefully, one day you will come to the discovery that all that we purport to be and to do are fragments of a dream, enthralled as one is by the siren song of the "I"-

thought. Our entire individual existence is nothing but a figment of the imagination. But don't take my word for it. Find out for yourself through your own self-inquiry and don't give up until you have got to the bottom of this thing. In this connection, the Buddha's first words after his enlightenment experience were: "Desire, I know thy root, from imagination art thou born; no more shall I indulge in imagination, I shall have no desire anymore." Much in the same vein, Nisargadatta proclaimed: "Be empty of all mental content, of all imagination and effort, and the very absence of obstacles will cause reality to rush in." The ultimate conclusion is that the highest teaching is no-teaching, nothing that one can "do," only to *be* and remain silent so that the Silent Mind, which is the State of No-Mind, may reveal everything. For us, who for our entire lives have been accustomed to manipulating and "controlling" things in one way or another, this is indeed most unusual and arduous. So restless and indomitable is the mind, and the bad habits we have fallen into! The colloquialism "wait and see!" acquires a new and vibrant meaning, that of "Be still, yet watchful to whatever may be revealed."

You are right that my own books represent a concerted effort of thought, without which I would have had nothing to offer. But you oversimplify the situation. Not only thought is present, but also meditation on the thoughts and finally an apperception of what *is*. In this apperception, thought and concept play no role whatsoever. Thus, one begins with thought; thought turns into itself, and one ends with no-thought, or the condition of

No-Mind — that is, if the *vichara* has been effective. And whatever conclusions one arrives at within thought serve only to emasculate thought in toto! One might call this the triumph of insight over thought. And since the "person" is essentially brought about and kept alive by the concept — the image of an entity within the realm of thought — the result is the ending of what previously served as a center of thought, speech and action. What remains is an Emptiness, pure Consciousness, which is the Self of all sentient beings.

I agree with you that there is no place of dogmatism in all this, that a certain flexibility is desirable to accommodate different grades of comprehension, but that does not include selling out the truth. That I will never do for the sake of appearing reasonable and amenable. Whatever truth is perceived, it must not be watered down, not even to make it more palatable or comprehensible to the masses. This is no elitism but Self-preservation in the highest sense of the word.

You are talking about helping others. But who are the others? Are there any others? You see, this is where *advaita* demands total and clear vision, and then is absolutely non-compromising, for we are touching on its essence: There are no others to help! Helping oneSelf, one helps all beings in the Universe, for the simple reason that Self comprises all beings and non-beings. Fortunately or unfortunately, there is no meeting ground between dualism and non-dualism. So-called "helping" others while in the state of duality may or may not be beneficial to these "others." Helping on the relative level is one matter, helping on the ultimate level from a timeless perspective is another. I suggest that we do all we can to help on the immediate, physical level, but always keep in mind our limitations from a wider perspective. To truly help another in a spiritual sense, the best we can do is to realize our true nature. There is no greater gift that can be offered to the world.

But just one thing here: I don't see anything wrong with imagination. After all, you yourself in your books are fond of using "thought experiments," and what are thought experiments other than imagination?

No, the imagination that the Buddha and others talk about is a thought projection driven by desire or fear, or it represents the mere rambling of a mind out of control, not the "imagination" exercised in the practice of science or the arts, which is of a totally different dimension.

A thought experiment is a properly thought-out scientific experiment that is, however, not feasible in practice but otherwise totally legitimate. So the experiment is carried out in the mind only, theoretically, and may result in some useful findings. To properly appreciate this kind of activity, I suggest you consult some physics text where examples of this practice are described.

8

TAKING ONE'S STAND IN THE ETERNAL

What is to be done about the conditioned mind?

From the point of view of realization, absolutely nothing. First, one must see that so long as the desire is there for changing one's conditioning, or even to "uncondition" oneself, one remains stuck — mired in duality. For what is it that induces one to do something about one's conditioning? Behind all such activity there is still a "doer," an entity that wants to change that which *is.* The energy represented by the "doer" is actually a subtle form of conditioning in itself. It puts in place an attenuated frame of reference. The inevitable conclusion is that any form of "doing" cannot help but perpetuate the problem. In this connection, mere *seeing* is everything.

In practice, what you consider your far-away ideal of the "unconditioned mind" is only a mind in which one form of conditioning has been replaced by another, possibly more subtle, form of conditioning. You may change your conditioning a bit and thereby perhaps make life somewhat more bearable, as is endeavored in psychoanalysis, but if you want self-realization, leave your mind alone. Go beyond, or rather before, the mind.

The body, mind and senses are all perceived as objects, by something other. This indicates that you are not body, mind and senses but are, in fact, that other, which perceives everything as object but is not an object in itself. Instead, it is the only true Subject; since only objects can be perceived, it cannot see itself just as an eye cannot see itself.

Therefore, pay no more attention to body and mind than is absolutely necessary, since they are not your real self. Realize that they have a life of their own, and that their activities are entirely mechanical, deterministic, solely governed by the dynamics of action-and-reaction. The very fact that they appear before you as manifestation, means that you are not that manifestation; that which observes the conditioned entity cannot possibly be the conditioning. When the identification with the conditioned entity ceases, there is an immediate stepping out of time, out of both conditioning and unconditioning. To see all this clearly destroys any form of identification with the false; then what remains is only the real, your true self. Just be that always.

A primary requirement for the spiritual life, as I understand it, is freedom from all attachments. But now in practice, I have found it extremely difficult to free myself from all sorts of attachments that I have become aware of recently. In fact, I have found it is not really possible to do so, at least for myself; and I believe the same applies to almost everyone else. What have you got to say about this?

Once an attachment has been formed, I agree it is virtually impossible to free oneself. That is, if one takes the conventional approach of struggling from attachment towards detachment. Almost all of us concentrate our attention on the object of attachment. We practice "detachment" from the point of view of a subject that is taken for granted, an individuality that at some early date has been imposed on us and been uncritically accepted. Now what I propose is to give fullest attention, not to the object of our attachment or that which enslaves us, but to the "attacher," the entity that experiences the attachment. If one does that, one will see that the attachment ensues not from the object, however desirable or alluring it may appear, but from the entity to whom it appears. An entirely new vista appears with this radically different point of view: All exists only within the "experiencer." I see that at some time in the past I was clothed in Form, and what needs to be done is take off this clothing and return to the naked state, which is the purity of my essence prior to space and time, prior to body-mind. Then see if there is still any attachment left.

How did you personally get the first intimation and insight into non-duality?

As a youngster — I must have been about thirteen — I did have some spontaneous experiences by which there was a kind of experience of nothingness; that is, I had disappeared as the "me" which I had provisionally known, and it and everything else had merged into one field, one background, it might be said. These experiences gave me some foretaste of the state of the Ultimate or the Totality, but without as yet much understanding as to what was going on. Later, when I seriously began to face the question "Who Am I?," I obtained a somewhat deeper understanding of a more rational kind of the nature of that "me" and the source from which it had arisen.

I subsequently became increasingly clear about the incontrovertible truth of what I had read in spiritual writings as "non-duality" or *advaita.* First of all, I became convinced, by direct insight, into the spurious reality of what I had carried with me since my earliest conscious days, the idea of being a "me." It is really quite simple. What proof is there that the "I" exists as a separate entity? That is the key question here. Everything else depends on that affirmation. With the "I" affirmed, there is inevitably "you," "he," and "it," or the entire world of objects — more succinctly, the "world."

Now what makes us talk about "I" and think there is an independent "person" as the referent? That is where body, mind and senses come in; through their combined action we come up with the statement and conceptualization of "I am." In other words, there is sensation, then thought and finally naming. In more detail, the body is perceived through the sense organs, conceptualized and pronounced to be a "body," where the latter concept already implies boundaries and so separation. Indeed, the whole of this process may be said to be an act of thought, which we have accepted as being the final arbiter in determining our reality. The weakness in the argument is that there is no independent authority to affirm it. For who is accepting, confirming if you will, the finding that this body-mind entity is for real? It is that same body-mind entity, that very same empirical reality, of course! It is the only reference system at my disposal, in which everything is being measured. Therefore, one is begging the question or making a circular argument when stating "I am." In actual fact, there is only sensation and thought, but even that cannot be confirmed independently! Any certainty one can have is only mental. And what really is "mental"? All that is, all that was and all that will ever be is of the nature of mental construct or "appearance." It is just as in looking at a hologram, one observes certain shapes and forms that we can designate as recognizable "objects," but that have no real grounding. The true Ground of our being lies beyond all that and is nameless and totally outside the world of experience. I am reminded of a remark once made by Krishna Menon when asked about the significance of reincarnation. He replied that one dies with every thought or feeling, and so one lives many lives even within a short period of time! In other words, one is only aware of being "someone," of "having a life," during an act of thinking! Otherwise, there is no change in us, no living or dying as opposite states. From the body-mind point of view, there are discontinuities, different bodies and different lives. But from the point of view of Consciousness, beyond identification with a particular body, there is an utterly different state. There is no longer *my* thought and *your* thought, this present life and my next life or past life, but a state of timeless and spaceless Eternity. Upon my death, I am not really affected; there is no exit, nor was there ever an entry point or so-called "birth," only a particular body appears, lingers for some time and drops away. The Consciousness does not leave me, because I ever *am* that Consciousness. When we talk about "he lost consciousness," it is rather the other way around: "Consciousness lost him." True death is not even a theoretical possibility, because my being as Consciousness does not permit its opposite, Unconsciousness, to exist: the Self or Consciousness, by definition, is that which lies totally beyond all pairs of opposites. Part of our difficulty is that we are so easily led astray by the limitations of words, their everyday meanings, and our inability to transcend them.

When one truly sees and accepts this vision of our real nature completely and unreservedly, one takes one's stand in the Eternal. Then one can only fall silent; the whole of our ordinary so-called life experience is seen to be nothing but a series of mind-games — a juggling with projected images, with the "juggler" himself being only a mere image among images. All our certainties are seen to be like footprints in the sky! The only reality that emerges from all this is the Consciousness or the Self, upon which all sensation and thought is projected. This is how I came to my first basic recognition of the truth of *advaita*.

9

Religious Beliefs, Morality and Spiritual Truth

It seems strange to me that after all these thousands of years so many different religions are still vying with one another in expounding the Truth, and that a consensus in the matter has never developed. After all, there is only one truth. And why is it that, notwithstanding all that missionary activity in the world, no religious activity, collectively, has been able to effect a fundamental change in the condition of man?

Just as one can find different scientific theories which describe the Universe, each being internally consistent and having some correspondence to reality, yet none of them being totally satisfactory in all respects, so it is with the various symbolic representations of reality within the religious sphere. Some may be more refined or more widely acceptable than others, all having a certain validity, yet none is totally adequate in achieving religion's professed goal of transforming man and creating a better world. The reason is that religion as well as philosophy and science are all on the verbal level, whereas truth is ever on the much deeper nonverbal level and thereby incommunicable; it has to be experienced directly, in silence.

Let me put this in other words: both science and religion deal with "models" of reality — that is, abstractions of that which is essentially non-abstractable. For any abstraction of what *is* implies a taking away, a reduction, introducing a limitation to make it graspable by the intellect. Ultimately, therefore, both the scientific and the religious paths, in efforts at pinning down the "final truth," can be no more than so much "piffle before the wind."

So it may be said that what *is* may be easily perceived and lived with, without producing conflict, when all efforts by man to represent his understanding in the form of scientific or religious models — mere grist for the mill of the intellect — are dropped. In a wider context, this means that what *is* should be allowed simply to be without being made into concept. For as soon as what *is* has been conceptualized, thought-desire sets to work on it to produce "what *should be*," and a center or "individual" with his many likes and dislikes comes alive. This is not the usual cause-and-effect process; the reverse is equally valid: the center of conditioning brings about the concepts of what *is* and what *should be*. Both events happen instantaneously — the birth of the "person" and the conceptualization of what *is* through thought-memory. In their absence or avoidance, there is no longer the concept of what *should be*: there is only the real, the pure undifferentiated light of the "I am" consciousness, and nothing else is wanted anymore. Nor is there any longer anyone who could possibly do this "wanting."

I have heard you say that mankind has continually lived with a crisis in consciousness, and throughout the ages only a few people have faced the issue. Why so few?

Because most people don't want to pay the price when they see a little bit of what is entailed — the giving up of all their comfortable positions in life. All their vested interests are at stake, and they are painfully aware of that. When faced with this tremendous giving up that is involved, they say to themselves: "I can't do it. I want to hang on to my cherished beliefs." They feel insecure without all that which they have been using as a crutch. So they simply won't pursue it.

Where does Morality fit into your scheme of things?

Not greatly, at least not as a primary spiritual truth. First of all, the one who has realized himself does not need Morality, with its imposed rules of behavior, for he functions in his natural state, which is always inherently moral, and more than that, surpasses Morality. Morality, therefore, would seem to be applicable and useful only in the state of ignorance. But there one finds it is practically impotent. Take the case of the ordinary man who does not know who he is. Considering himself to be the body, he expects to be in the world for a certain duration and then disappear from it. In his condition, the world naturally appears as a hostile place, and his ultimate sense of morality is essentially self-survival — that is, survival of his imagined identity. Anything else, any values superimposed on that, will only be a thin veneer. And logically, since any system of imposed morality is relative, artificial, he may calculate that he can commit antisocial acts with impunity. Consciously or unconsciously, he reckons that if he can manage not to be caught within his life span, he goes scot-free, because after that there is nothing.

So why bother with enforcing morality? What is its value? Only as a self-protective device for Society, but as a religious or spiritual precept it has limited value. The only value it can be said to have is to curtail the ego, to give it some sense of its own limits — which, in a few cases, might lead to its inward turning and self-discovery. But from an ultimate point of view, we must never forget that an "imposed morality" is always inherently unstable and really a contradiction in terms — for it is basically "immorality," just as an assumed virtue is no virtue at all.

Is there then no place at all for espousing, not imposing or enforcing, certain moral guidelines to a student of advaita*?*

Up to a point, there is, but only up to that point. Morality applies solely in the ignorant stage. "Good" and "bad" are always relative values; there are no absolutes here. Within an empirical scale of values, however, I could define "good" as such behavior that brings a person nearer to discovering his true nature; and "bad" as all such behavior that takes him further away from it. And since our actions are determined by the underlying thoughts, I would further say that "virtue" flows from a mind that has turned inward, is inclined to self-examination, and non-virtue is of a mind that has lost contact with its roots, is carried away by and ever reacting to the stimuli of this world.

It must be apparent that these moral values apply only to the seeker, the *sadhaka*, not to the *jnani*. The rules of morality cannot logically apply to the *jnani*, for (by definition) the *jnani* has lost his individuality. So, who is there to practice morality? The *jnani*, it can be said, reflects the morality inherent in what *is*. He represents the values of reality, the Infinite, since he is just that, and these values cannot be measured by a finite yardstick.

Since both "virtue" and "non-virtue" are strictly relative within the scale of moral values, I have used the term "non-virtue" rather than "sin," which has an absolute connotation. On a more advanced level, virtue can be said to manifest when the thought is no longer based on "identity" — name and form — or on the "I"-thought; non-virtue, on the other hand, is still an elaboration of the interplay of entities in space and time.

10

REINCARNATION — FACT OR FICTION?

Some sages say reincarnation is a fact; others say it is all a lot of nonsense. There are also examples of sages who at one time affirm it, and at other times speak out against it. What is one to make of all that?

Forget about the sages. Find out for yourself. The sages speak only to one's individual level of maturity, the individual capacity to understand. That is why they are loath to give answers in general terms, for fear of being misunderstood.

Before tackling the question in depth, we should first be clear about the meaning of the term "reincarnation," understand it fully on the semantic level. The answer to any problem always lies in the question, in our particular terms of reference.

Let us go into the term "re-incarnation," intentionally spelled with a hyphen, so that we are forced to look at the root meaning of the word. In the first place: Is there "incarnation"? Of course, there is such a thing; otherwise we would not be talking about re-incarnation. We obviously have accepted "incarnation." The entire world of living creatures is a form of incarnation, is it not? "Incarnate" derives from the Latin word *incarnari*, literally meaning "to be made flesh"; in other words, "embodied." All human beings are in the flesh, so we have all been incarnated, right? But then the inevitable next question must be: What is it that has been "incarnated"?

All human beings have a sense of self, because all say constantly "I," pointing to something beyond the flesh, and human beings constantly appear on the world scene and disappear from it, so there ever is "incarnation" upon their birth and "decarnation," if I may coin that term, upon physical dissolution or death. Now depending on whether I emphasize the phenomenon of incarnation just described as a momentary fact or a continuous process, I term it "incarnation" or "reincarnation." I am justified to use the latter term if I wish to emphasize the never-ceasing nature of the phenomenon.

Until now we have simply observed, and proceeded carefully from fact to fact by restating the obvious, as it were. And in doing so, we have come to some understanding of what is meant by reincarnation. Now, the "reincarnationists" have done something entirely different; they have gone well beyond this point and made several important assumptions and passed them off as proven fact. They have superimposed a theory which pleases them; that is, by postulating that re-incarnation is occurring through manifestation as essentially the same, unchanging entity, or self, they have given themselves continuity beyond the grave. So we are back to the fundamental question: What do we mean by self? If your understanding has it that you are a particular, unchanging entity, which alone would validate the concept of a particular identity, you would be entitled to make this the basis for a theory of reincarnation. But then the onus for proving its underlying assumption would still be on you. If, on the other hand, you apperceive the self as a non-duality, as being beyond the realm of space-time or "multiplicity," then although you may still use the term "reincarnation," your understanding of its significance will be quite different. You realize that "individuals" come about through the interplay of an infinite number of combinations and permutations of the same building blocks but that it is never the same person who manifests as incarnation. Thus, to discover the truth of the matter independently of what someone else maintains, one should find out what that "self" is that everlastingly "incarnates."

From this point onwards, one is completely on one's own, for this is the very point that ratiocination or intellectual persuasion can go no further. Because at this stage one first has to go into one's alleged identity. And obviously only you can tell who you are; nobody else can do that for you.

My conviction is that the self is indivisible, the totality. Upon death, manifestation through that persona or mask ceases totally; that mask is irretrievably lost upon the psychosomatic dissolution called "death." The concepts of past, present and future are mere illusions based on memory, which depends on a somatic base. For without memory, where is re-cognition? And without re-cognition, where is the past and where is the projected future? With the dissolution of that base, there is only the Eternal or the Timeless, which does not admit of even a trace of continuity. Only the non-dual self remains and ever is; thus, I have proved to my own satisfaction that there are no individual, lasting entities to be sequentially incarnated. There ever exists only my present incarnation. I must therefore reject the concept of "reincarnation" as commonly propagated by its adherents. There is only the Self, whose manifestation is eternally now. That manifestation is like a flame which seems to be continuous and steady through time, yet upon closer examination is found to be totally intangible, being an entirely new flame consisting of different, evanescent fuel particles at every moment of its existence.

Second, inquire to whom the thoughts, emotions, feelings, etc. occur; in other words: What is the background, the screen, upon which our objective world appears? And who is the subject who knows all this manifestation, the Ultimate Knower? You talk about immortality, but our entire psychological functioning takes place in time and space; it is nothing but movement in memory. All thoughts deal only with the past and the future, yet living is ever in the present, the Now. If you affirm your immortality, then you should have discovered that part of you which is not bound by time and space. Have you, through your own deep inquiry, discovered your real self? Only that which exists eternally is real: "I am."

There seems to be a lot of confusion around reincarnation or rebirth. Some of the greatest spiritual thinkers seem to have an ambiguous attitude: sometimes considering reincarnation as true, other times denying its reality altogether. It is as though they are talking from both sides of their mouth, perhaps hedging their bets. What is one to make of all this? [The questioner happens to be a scientist, so the answer to the question is more specifically geared for his mind-set.]

If you expect a categorical answer from me — yes or no — you will be sorely disappointed. You may think I am hedging or I can't deal with the question, but that is not really the case. You see, my position is that no one can give such a yes or no type of answer, because it would imply a gross oversimplification. Such an answer would also be incorrect in a sense, for it would only tell part of the story. Certain subjects, especially those of a more fundamental nature, do not lend themselves to such treatment; they go beyond any semantics.

Let me explain this further. Since you have been educated as a scientist, I will adduce some analogies from that area. Take the nature of light. Experiments have shown that light has a dual aspect, sometimes exhibiting the properties of particles, other times those of electromagnetic waves, depending on how it is being studied. This is especially strange since particles and waves could not be more different from each other and are, in fact, practically opposites: particles are extremely small — highly concentrated packages of energy — whereas waves are spread out over an infinite expanse of space. Physicists, however, are no longer bothered by such conundrums; they now simply talk about light as being made up of "wavicles"; that is to say, it is both particulate and wave-like in nature. Like much in the new physics, it is beyond human intuition to grasp this concept, as it embraces contradictory elements; but, as I said, workers in this field have become inured to this phenomenon; they do not insist anymore on testing everything by means of linear thought or logic. It is almost as though they have let the door open for an occasional "act of faith." Since this new, utterly pragmatic approach has led to tangible results, it is no longer challenged by the orthodoxy in the scientific community.

Now why I have apparently digressed from the topic in hand is that I think a very similar situation prevails with respect to the subject of reincarnation or rebirth. On various grounds, it is possible to maintain totally opposite points of view, namely that reincarnation is a fact and also that there is and can be no such thing. So let's go into it in stages and look very carefully at the way the problem is formulated, since with most spiritual questions the answer is already contained in the question. In this case, it all depends on what level we are treating the subject, whether we are looking at it ontologically — that is, from the point of view of what actually *is*, the ultimate level — or whether we are treating it appearance-wise as relating to a psychosomatic entity. To clarify this, let's get back to the subject of light. Even on the level of elementary physics, we can discern a simple duality: light (more specifically, sunlight) can be considered as either "approximately white" or "yellow-white" — the way it appears to us — or as a melange of colors of infinite variety when passed through a prism. It all depends on what you take the real nature of light to be: before or after passing through the prism.

The point can be argued from either side and, in a sense, both points of view are correct, embracing both what *is* and the way it *appears*. We hasten to add, however, that this "what *is*" itself can be further viewed as consisting of another pair of "what *is*" and "what appears" on a deeper level. In this particular case, this is with respect to the meaning of color perception: focusing of light rays through the eye lens, stimulation of special color receptor cells in the retina, physiochemical changes in these cells, conduction of impulses through the optical nerve, physiochemical changes therein, parallel changes in consciousness (an unknown territory), interpretation through memory, etc. Generally, this kind of examination, a search for meaning on ever deeper levels, leads to a series of regressions, where the "what *is*" is split up each time into a further "what *is*" and "what appears." (Sometimes such regression can go on *ad infinitum.*) In the example given regarding the nature of light as "wavicles," this would require, first of all, a deeper exploration into the concepts of "particle" and "wave," in other words: What is traditionally meant by these terms?

Now it is just like that with reincarnation. When treating things on the most fundamental level, one frequently arrives at a paradox or an infinite regress — signs that the intellect has come to the end of its tethers, that we stand at the very edge of its range of applicability, and that a quantum leap is required for a breakthrough.

Let us see how this applies with respect to rebirth. Paradoxically, both statements — reincarnation is real and is not real — have some validity, depending on the point of view of the observer and the level on which he treats the subject. If you consider yourself, as most of us do, as a distinct person, an independent psychosomatic entity, then yes, there may well be a return of that entity in some shape or other. Certainly with respect to the psychosomatic potential or the vital energy representing or underlying the person, its preservation can be accepted. It is a well-established fact that, although everything is subject to continual change, essentially nothing in nature gets destroyed. Just as one cannot get something out of nothing, the opposite also applies: one cannot get nothing out of something. This means then that when something is there, *in one form or another* that something remains in existence, whether it is recognizable as such or not. This posited persistence of the "something" that accompanies the "individual" may well constitute a generalization of the well-known law in physics of the conservation of mass-energy. The latter states that no matter in what quantities mass and energy are converted into each other or in whatever way they are distributed throughout space-time, nothing ever gets lost; the total mass-energy in the universe remains constant.

Thus, we may say that even if the "individual" perishes, its basic physical constituents, as well as the pure energy representing that psychosomatic entity (Nisargadatta's "vital air" or "life force"), will persist. As we have discussed before in these meetings, the material elements of which we are composed are the approximately hundred chemical elements of western science or the five basic elements of Hinduism — it comes to much the same thing — put together in an infinite number of combinations and permutations under the influence of the three *guṇas* or "basic qualities." On the purely somatic level, the mechanism is being understood through the science of genetics, the way the body gives continuity to itself — a process that has evolved from the simple splitting in two of protozoa and other unicellular organisms.

Now it may be argued that the preservation of the elements constituting the individual does not necessarily validate rebirth, if by that term we mean the exact holding together in a fixed pattern of the individual's components through different cycles. Here, obviously, the nature of the individual must first be clarified.

Sri Nisargadatta Maharaj, on one of the rare occasions that he discussed the subject on the highest level, stated that rebirth can be said to be a fact, *but it is not the same individual that is reborn.* Which naturally again leads us to the fundamental question: What is meant by the "individual"? To have any meaning at all, the entity must be — and survive as — a fixed configuration of the elements of which it is composed; only in that case could we admit the possibility or likelihood of rebirth. Accepting Maharaj's aforementioned statement, that a *different* individual is reborn, the question then arises:

Can it still be named "rebirth," since the prefix "re-" requires repetition of what preceded, entailing an exact replica of the previous entity.

But also a second, perhaps more important question comes to the fore: If one accepts that it is not the same individual — that is, the same configuration of the entity's building stones — that returns, then is there really any essential difference between a so-called reborn individual and the individual in his present incarnation? If one's present life is only a projection of images in total flux or a "dream," and the next life that very same dream recycled, what is the point in, and what do we mean by, differentiating between the two? And, more to the point, *how* could one differentiate between the two? A recycled dream is still only a dream. And also, *who* is to make such differentiation? That could naturally only be a third dream. Those who wish for rebirth should find out if they can clearly identify those parts of themselves that they wish to preserve.

Some vaguely familiar items may occasionally stand out in the dream due to residual memory — experienced as an occasional "déjà vu" by many of us — but that is all. In a rare case, perhaps even more than a few small fragments may register; but it is still a far cry from maintaining that it is the same individual that has returned. Or that it even concerns an "individual" at all! I would say it is rather the interaction of certain residual engrams or shards of memory. In this connection, J. Krishnamurti, on one of the rare occasions that he dealt with the subject of memory in some depth, maintained that memories stand on their own, that they are not held within any container but stick together naturally through mutual attraction and not through being controlled by an entity or individual. In other words, there are memories but there is no "rememberer" or "recognizer."

Thus, what appears as some fixed entity with a definite and permanent identity is, on closer examination, to be seen as something at once much more fluid and more indeterminate. It is therefore difficult to differentiate between the individual as he is in this present incarnation and as he possibly may reappear in "his"(?) next one. So it will be seen that the question of reincarnation can indeed be answered in two opposing ways, depending entirely on one's point of view. It is analogous to the apparently different statements: "the glass is half-full" and "the glass is half-empty." Both statements are essentially correct; which particular expression is used depends entirely on one's point of view.

More generally then, one may state that whether it concerns particles or waves, sentient beings "to-be-born-only-once" or "to-be-recycled-into-eternity," the nature of physical light or that of the spiritual Light — the Light of Awareness — it cannot be adequately explained through concept and thought. The deepest reality can never be articulated through mere words. Whenever we try, immediately warning signs appear in the form of paradox, infinite regress and such indicators. In fact, the very appearance of contradiction serves as an important signal that alerts us to the need for transcending all familiar concepts and verbal inadequacies.

Recapitulating, it can be said it all depends upon the perceiver and his approach. Just as those who investigated light in one particular way found it to consist of particles and those who investigated it in another way found it to be waves, so those who can only perceive the world dualistically will see that world inhabited by separate entities that can undergo rebirth because these "entities" exhibit a more or less rigid structure. On the other hand, for those who have transcended duality, reality is not visualized as being composed of rigid patterns or separate entities; to them the question of rebirth has become moot. They realize that this self — composed of space and time — is nothing more than an appearance, a fleeting dream. On that level, as appearance, the possibility of a re-appearance or rebirth is granted — even though it is not clear exactly what that re-appearance would comprise — but since they deny reality to mere appearance, they will not view things through the concept of rebirth. For them, the "individual" does not really exist as such; at any time, there is only Life and no one who lives it. Since there is no structure to replicate, there cannot be any question of a return or rebirth. They are looking beyond to the Source of all appearances, the unchanging background against which all change is perceived. For them, the Self is not a mere appearance; it is the Changeless, beyond space-time, immortal.

11

Conversation on Vulnerability, Criminality, Memory, Crazy Wisdom, Sacred Art, and Other Topics

(Verbatim record of an interview conducted by Messrs. Rick Moore and Cortland Harris, of The Claremont Forum, *Claremont, California, in the summer of 1993 at La Jolla, California. Since 1995, the Forum incorporates* The Prison Library Project, *which continues the work of Bo and Sita Lozoff, who for years have introduced prisoners around the world to yoga and meditation.)*

The Claremont Forum: Did you ever meet Sri Nisargadatta Maharaj?

Robert Powell: I never met the man. I had planned to visit him the very year he passed away, but for personal reasons was not able to do so. Maharaj succumbed to throat cancer, from which he had been suffering for some years. He was a member of a succession of spiritual teachers, the *Navanath Sampradaya*, all of whom were householders.

Although it would no doubt have been beneficial to have seen him, I was not destined to do so and in a way, I am not too distressed about it. You see, my approach is probably somewhat different from that of the average devotee. My main interest has always been the philosophy of *advaita*, of which Maharaj is one of several exponents and to which there are various, non-exclusive approaches. Here the word "philosophy" does not really convey what I mean, for *advaita* is more a way of liberation, an utterly fresh way of living. Do you know the etymology of this term *advaita*? It literally means "not-two" or "non-duality." What it connotes is that our usual vision of ourselves, and the way we live in society, is completely mistaken. The way we function at the moment is as separate entities, each of us being an island unto ourselves. All the other members of society are separate and in many ways competing with us; this is one of the main reasons why there is strife and sorrow in the world. There is nothing that unites us except concepts, which are theoretical and have no actual reality.

Now in *advaita* you come to a vision of yourself and the world in which there is Oneness; each of us is the Totality in which there is no scope for separate entities or "individualities." The only way to arrive at such an insight is to turn inward and find out who you really are — not what you have imbibed from your parents, educators, the world at large and your heritage. For all that is merely conceptual, based entirely on hearsay that one has absorbed without questioning. Therefore, what is needed is a revolution in one's outlook which, in turn, may lead to a corresponding revolution in one's functioning.

In India the guru-disciple relationship is an empirical system, which has been developed to facilitate this end and which was found to have certain results. Ideally, the relationship may lead to a transfer of understanding and Grace from the teacher to the student. And Grace is always necessary to convert the newly acquired understanding of the student into actual transformation of his self. However, a warning should be issued here. For, in extreme cases where the student is blindly attached to the guru, this can actually become a hindrance in bringing about the required revolution in consciousness. One can see this happening quite a lot, especially with Westerners who don't fully understand the mechanism of the guru-disciple relationship. For example, when the disciple develops a strong personal attachment to the guru, it may inhibit him in coming to that inward turning.

CF: The energy is all focused outwardly?

RP: The relationship then is all a form of adulation. Being miserable with himself, the disciple clings to something that he feels is greater and nobler — and that is the guru. But often the guru does not measure up to the student's ideal. Thus, we have all these scandals today with unscrupulous gurus, especially those who have come to the West recently. Not all, but certain gurus have formed exploitative relationships with their students, and these can be very dangerous.

But otherwise, the disciple can have a healthy relationship with the guru, if he has a genuine interest to discover himself; then the guru can serve as a catalyst in the process of self-discovery.

CF: I see a real pervasiveness in the relationships with those teachers who have come to the West in which the student doesn't have the necessary self-confidence to trust his own perceptions to follow the method you speak of.

RP: It requires confidence and earnestness, and also persistence. You may have confidence in the beginning and you are all fascinated by the process, but it takes a lot more than that because there are so many distractions, competing interests, so many temptations. The world is full of diversions for the spiritual aspirant, so it is very difficult to stay the course. One can, for instance, be overwhelmed by political and financial events or by personal relationships, family affairs. All this is very easy to happen, because there is a tremendous fascination or magnetism in these outward relationships. To turn inward in the face of all this, and to say that all that is secondary because what I am is something much more basic than all that goes on in the world — the fight for power, money, and the competitiveness it breeds — takes a lot of energy and sticking to the quest. Yet, once one has gone a little distance along this path, one begins to realize it is the only sane way to live. It is either that or you succumb to all the pressures of the world and are crushed by them . . . unless you are extremely lucky and have some apparent security, perhaps because you are financially well-off or are part of an influential group of people. But even in that case, when it comes to ultimate values, you still have to face death, the question of coming to an end. And we all know that many ambitious people who have succeeded in the world have not been able to face that. Because it means the ultimate destruction of all they have amassed and worked for so assiduously.

So it comes back to values. Do we live by the values of society or do we live by the values of what *is* . . . of Reality? Reality has its own set of values, but you have to discover first what they are. For that, you have to understand what makes you tick, the nature of that so-called "individuality," or ego. Anything else is useless and irrelevant. And that was the great thing about Nisargadatta; he always came straight to the point: "Find out what you are, who you are. Then, after that we will talk."

CF: In this looking within, how do you see the role of, say, a *bhakta*, who is on the devotional path?

RP: There is the devotional path (*bhakti*) and that of *jnana*. The latter term means "knowledge," but it isn't knowledge as an accumulation of facts and relationships, as in science. It is a special kind of knowledge which goes beyond all conventional knowledge and is not based on memory. It comes only through self-knowing.

In *bhakti*, which is devotional in the sense that you discard all self-concern and self-importance, you absorb whatever you can from the guru to the extent of regarding him as all-knowing, a Godhead, as it were. This is all right if the teacher has integrity, since in such relationship there is the beginning of a giving up of oneself, the ego, and even more of a giving up *on* oneself. If one has that relationship of veneration and absorption from the teacher, then one's own self becomes much less important and one is open to something from beyond oneself. That, in essence, is the *bhakti* approach.

Jnana has a little more content in its approach, requiring a great deal of insight, to start with. However, the interesting thing is that at some point the *bhakti* and *jnana* paths merge and become one and the same. To understand how this can be, *bhakti* is surrender, total and unconditional, and *jnana* is giving up one's knowledge, the entire analytical process. But on the ultimate level, the ego is exactly that sum-total of all that one clings to and is identified with as knowledge and experience. So both approaches amount to the same thing in the end: a total letting go of the past, of all content of consciousness. There is no more separation between the paths and one can no longer call it *bhakti* or *jnana*, or whatever; there is something that is unmentionable. You cannot classify it any longer.

CF: Can you speak a little bit about vulnerability, and where that comes in?

RP: You have to be absolutely vulnerable, totally open to receive the intimations from your Source. If you isolate yourself through building various defenses, you miss. You cannot cut yourself off from the Real, and the Real can be painful. It *must* be painful because it stands in direct opposition to all one's little vested interests, all the things that we cherish because society tells us they are important and desirable. And if you believe those things and you cling to them, then you become hardened and create a shell around yourself, composed of those values that you try to defend. But that is just where the problem lies in the first place. Because really there is no difference between society and yourself. Our ignorance about ourselves is reflected in the consciousness, the very structure of society. We constantly project our ignorance of ourselves onto society and vice versa; so society is all the time reinforcing our ignorance, which is a really tragic situation and something that is not easy to escape from; it's like a vicious circle.

CF: So *advaita* would be something like a sword cutting directly at the root of the problem?

RP: You must cut at the root. You have to come to that point, and the sooner the better. Ignorance starts with the basic misconception of humanity that each of us is "somebody," who is born and will die. One sees the body and identifies with it. That is where the basic mistake comes in — our original sin, as it were, the identification with a physical form.

CF: Is it not the body that ultimately becomes vulnerable and sensitive to the intimation of the Self?

RP: No, not the body, ever. What is the body? It would not be, not manifest itself but for the grace of Consciousness; and without sentience the body is only an inert lump of matter. We are always making an artificial separation between the body and the mind and the Consciousness, but they are all interrelated: all is in Consciousness.

CF: There is a phrase that Nisargadatta always used in his talks to the effect of not worrying so much about the body; it takes care of itself, pretty much below the conscious level.

RP: It's not only that, not to worry about the body, but there is also the fact that one cannot do much about influencing it. We are deceiving ourselves when we think we can control and manipulate the body-mind entity. For what is it that thinks it can control and manipulate? It is only body-mind — a veritable circular argument. What else could it be? It is a trap, and this thinking can only give rise to conflict. Whatever happens is ordained to happen; it is your *prarabdha*. It is very subtle; even the fact that both you and I have become interested in these questions . . . . It is not that this has happened through an act of Will, but it just happened because it had to happen. There is a certain inevitableness about everything. We think that we are a separate entity that has Will, the power of action, but that is just our delusion. There is nobody who lives, we are "being lived," as it were. And you have to approach all of life from this understanding.

You just have to be aware of what goes on, that is all you can do. But to think you can manipulate that which goes on is a falsehood. You can only observe it, watch it, and then the watching itself may cause a change. When you just watch, without wanting to interfere, you see things from a different perspective, from the point of view of pure witnessing that has no vested interests. Witnessing is inherent in consciousness itself, the highest Consciousness spelled with a capital C. But the consciousness of body-mind processes is of a very much lower order. That is just like a machine, purely reactive. Some have designated it as *Mayaic*. Maharaj characterized it as the product of the five elements and the three *gunas* (basic qualities). These elements combine with one another in infinite combinations and permutations under the influence of these *gunas*. What this signifies is that it concerns a strictly mechanical, impersonal process, although we think we are such great persons. And the apparent personality that you and I present to others, it just happens. You may try to change some aspect of the personality, but even that is still only happening. On that level, you cannot put yourself outside the movement of life. The only way you can be beyond this mechanical process is when you are purely the Consciousness, the Absolute or the *parabrahman* — which is that which never changes, and is therefore not in space-time.

CF: Robert, you have been very supportive of *The Claremont Forum* over the last few years. Could you speak about why you have lent your support?

RP: I think "The Claremont Forum", through its branch, "The Prison Library Project", is doing important work in helping incarcerated people face the world and also themselves. They are totally cut off from the society, doing time. But actually they have a marvelous opportunity which the average free man or woman does not have, because the prisoners are cut off from all routine activities: the need to make money, trying to get somewhere in the world . . . . So in a sense this provides an opportunity — even though one may be disadvantaged, deprived . . . for turning inward, which is essential for knowing oneself. And that is where I think the *CF* can do a lot of good . . . . That is one aspect of it. The other is that, in a sense, we are all "doing time." So in the deepest sense, the inmates are no worse off than we are because there is tremendous pressure in the way that we, the so-called "free," live. We are always striving to do something, achieve something. We are always in a hurry, which is another shackle, and there is no way in which, if one lives in this society and not in an ashram or prison, one can escape from that pressure and not be a victim of it. Everyone of us in a way is held prisoner, and there is nothing we can do about it — always trying to get to a higher level of happiness, never satisfied with what *is* in the present moment. That is why I maintain we are all "doing time." This makes for a life of constant struggle, constant friction — always looking for gratification, whether it be through drugs, sex, or whatever, and psychologically through becoming "somebody," because essentially we cannot live with what we are. That is the crux of the matter, since we do not know ourselves. Once you know who you are, there is no question of satisfaction or dissatisfaction any longer. Then, you are satisfied with just having your basic needs met: eating, drinking, sex, etc. Few of us in the world can make use of the passive condition to free ourselves from doing time. It is ironic that those who are forced into doing time have the best opportunity to get out of it (doing time), while not actually being out of that cell.

CF: So whether we are talking about a physical prison or the prison every one of us lives in daily, you don't see much distinction?

RP: Exactly! We live in our internal prisons and, to my mind, the Prison Library Project can play an extremely valuable part in showing the way out.

CF: Robert, I would like you to comment on a quote from Carl Jung, if you would, and it goes something like this: "All neurosis is the avoidance of legitimate suffering."

RP: I don't quite understand what he means by "legitimate" suffering. I don't think there is any such division between legitimate and illegitimate suffering. All pain, both physical and mental, is a wake-up call, a signal that something is wrong. Basically, and putting it very bluntly, suffering is part of the condition of being a separate entity. And until you come to that point that you fully understand what you are, suffering is necessarily part of your being. There is no division between valid and invalid suffering. Being a separate entity is suffering. Until that separation goes and the entity disappears, you will be exposed to suffering. But once you have transcended the limitations of that separate entity, you may experience physical suffering and be subject to the various turmoils of the world, but you will be in a different state and no longer affected by the inner conflict of duality. For duality is conflict. It would be very nice if we could be in duality and have no suffering, but that would be somewhat like having your cake and eating it, too.

CF: What does compassion mean to you?

RP: True compassion is through non-duality, when you *are* the other. There is no division between the other and yourself; then compassion is not a mere intellectual thing. But society has so much cultivated that division... In fact, society would not exist in its present form without it. Do you see the joke? The whole social structure would collapse. It is man's vested interest. Talk to the man in the street and you will see how he has been indoctrinated by that philosophy.

CF: That's addiction to conflict?

RP: Conflict, strife, yes. Not only that, but it is based on a competitive, exploitative relationship in which the rich and powerful maintain themselves at the expense of the less fortunate strata of society. But I am not advocating communism or any system like that, because those measures are based on coercion or regimentation. It must be a true psychological equalization in first instance, not a taking away from the rich and giving it to the poor. We have tried that and it does not work, because both parties are steeped in ignorance, and the misery will go on. Even if you gave all the wealth to the poor, would they know how to handle it? Soon new divisions would appear. So there are innumerable problems in our social system, and changing it on a purely socioeconomic basis is not viable. That is why I attach so much importance to the need for spiritual regeneration, because I believe from that will come a regeneration of society. It won't happen the other way.

You can't leave it up to the political "leaders" to create more happiness in the world. Happiness is an individual thing; actually, the collective does not even exist, it is just an abstraction. The only thing that exists is what you are — and that "you" embraces all of us, the entire humanity. As J. Krishnamurti has expressed it so pointedly, "You are the world."

CF: I feel that this economy, the troubles we are presently having, would afford a real opportunity for people to slow down, maybe turn towards cottage industry type of work, and take responsibility for their economic situation instead of merely collecting a paycheck every two weeks. That would afford more time for spiritual interests. And also, when we have material goods taken from us, through repossession in debt, and consolidation, that is kind of a discarding of the false, and the real then will have more of an opportunity to appear.

RP: But is it really happening this way? It may to some small extent, and it has been going on in the sixties and seventies, but today what we are seeing is people trying to keep their heads above water more than anything else. The husband is working, the wife is working, the children are helping in any ways they can; and still it is not enough. They are deeply in debt. There is no economic reserve any longer, because the families are fully employed — that is, those who have work. They are trying not to drown by working harder and harder, and there is no margin for error or bad luck. Consequently, what we see is people in Japan are collapsing over their desks, dying from overwork and the same thing is beginning to happen here. So there is no salvation in that direction.

CF: So you don't see any possibility for an improvement in our spiritual condition if there were a reconstruction of our economy?

RP: I don't see any salvation that way at all. And, economically, I see things not getting better for quite some time.

CF: Where would you like to see things go?

RP: On what level?

CF: Individually, educationally . . . Sometimes, when I hear you speak I could see how people could take your words and use it do nothing.

RP: To do nothing is very difficult, you know. I am not preaching Quietism but my conviction is that no conditioned action can ever bring about real change. Only action springing from love and full understanding can do so.

CF: Are you referring to the idea of effortless effort?

RP: Yes. The mind won't allow you to do nothing. Even if you do nothing body-wise, your mind is still furiously involved. So that is not possible, to do nothing.

CF: Maybe a way to rephrase it would be to give up in the sense of: I don't have any effect on the world, I don't have any social impact, so why bother?

RP: Yes, this happens. But looking at it from a wider point of view, it's nothing to be alarmed about, actually; it is just one of the things that happen because society is the way it is. It is a corrupt society; all kinds of extreme cases present themselves: there are people who are overworking and people who are just doing the minimum. What will come out of all this eventually, only God knows. If you try to find the answer on that level, the social level, again you are getting caught. Watch it, witness it, detach yourself from it and if you have a certain understanding of what makes you tick, then you will do the right things personally and societally, the right action, without any thought; it will come naturally and spontaneously. But don't try to become a do-gooder or a reformer on the political, social level. All that is foolishness from the ultimate point of view for one who is still groping in the dark. I'm not saying there is no place for social work and political activity — on the contrary, activity on that level must continue — but to the spiritual aspirant they are secondary in importance. Ignorant people may say this is "selfishness," but that is due to their lack of understanding, since the goal of the spiritual aspirant is actually the ultimate destruction of the ego.

CF: Is the limited success of social action because those cause-and-effect relationships have been set for some time now?

RP: Yes, to think that one is going to change all that is basing one's actions on the wrong assumptions. When the assumptions are wrong, then whatever you do from those assumptions is necessarily wrong too. And the revolution they are talking about on the social level is not a revolution at all. It is a mere modification. The whole history of mankind has been one of revolution — one after another — and yet basically we have not changed. We are still muddling along, trying this, and trying that.

We haven't worked out a perfect social system yet, if it is ever possible. Maharaj once said, "Even if you were to develop such an ideal society, it would not last because it would be unstable. It would soon disintegrate or turn into something else."

CF: Because it would not have the inherent tensions of opposites holding it up?

RP: No, it isn't that. "Perfection" is something that just does not exist, except as a concept, in our head. It is an idea we hang on to. So when we talk about a "perfect society," we are not talking about the real world. Now that you ask me, I have actually never given it a thought since we are talking pure theory, not reality: What is "perfect"? And what is a perfect society? The concept will vary with the observer. What one may call a perfect society, another may call a very imperfect society. What are one's yardsticks? We do not have yardsticks for a perfect society. Even to talk about it is only so much hot air.

But there is perfection in what *is*. And in that perfection, which is right here in the present, there is both good and bad. Both must be there. You can't have good by chopping off the bad. The two are intimately related. What you call "good" is only good in relation to what is "bad" or what you perceive as "bad." It is like "high" and "low," "big" and "small." Can anyone tell exactly where "small" turns into "big"? They obviously are one continuum. Therefore, the question about what is a perfect society is wrongly placed.

CF: Sc we are making false presumptions all the time, relating everything to the subjective "I"?

RP: Yes, because society is an extrapolation of what we are, and this subjective "I" or body-mind entity is all conditioning. Instead, we should be basing our life on a different "I," the only real "I," which is the *one and only* Subject, or Subjectivity, as Maharaj has called it, and is all that exists. This "I" lies prior to all conditioning and is that upon which the entire world of objects is projected; it is our real Self.

CF: In the Native American tradition, there is a strong sense of the give-away, which I think could be "languaged" as obligation. Could you address this idea?

RP: I don't really know much about the American Indian traditions. From the little I have heard about it, I know it is communal (tribal). We as a culture have lost this essential element, because we have been so conditioned by this urge for personal survival that it is alien to the typical Westerner. In a way, it is something that would come naturally to a spiritual community that attaches very little value to individual property and where there is true sharing and a being, functioning, on the non-individual level. Then there is not even any need for conscious sharing; your natural being *is* the sharing.

So what has one got to hang on to? If you see that you have nothing, that you are nothing in yourself, you will not try to hang on to anything. And then, inevitably, the problem of life and death is also transformed.

A very young child hasn't got all these concepts about doing something in the world or protecting what he's got. On the basic physiological level, yes, he has got that; it is nature's way of programming him for physical survival. But on the psychological level, he lives in total spontaneity. He laughs one moment and cries the next, because the thread of psychological continuity is not yet there. The mental framework of being "somebody," a name and working for its protection and respectability — all that has not been imposed yet. A child is the most "unrespectable" person in the world, because he has no respectability to defend. He does not know anything about it. All that has been inculcated; it's all appearance and hearsay.

So to answer your original question, yes, a truly spiritual person will naturally be attuned to the American Indian way of life.

CF: How do you see that obligation, if you will, showing up in our culture?

RP: I don't see it showing up! I think, to the vested interests, the power groups in society, this would pose quite a threat, this trend towards obligation to the less fortunate, the disadvantaged people in the world. The society is ridden with prejudice, not only racial and sexual, but also prejudices directed against all the weaker members of society. So its very being is at stake to maintain those strata: the people who have nothing and those who have all the power and who rise to the top. To come back to your Project: Why do we have criminals and crime? Partly, it could be pathological, that some of us have the wrong genes. Just like your body can be ill, so your mind can be ill if something goes wrong with your brain cells: lacking a few chemicals, you go crazy. This is proven medical knowledge. So you commit a criminal act and end up in a cell. And we treat these people differently, as though it is something that is attached to their "badness." But what is "badness"? Why do some people act badly and others have this real saintly manner? Nobody ever goes into that, coolly and analytically. And what is the nature of a saint, a Mother Theresa? To my mind, it is largely a matter of what in Sanskrit is called *prarabdha* or destiny. Most people bring in the idea of personal responsibility, which is not invalidated by our considerations, but there is obviously more to this question than meets the eye. Ultimately, things are the way they are. We will always have saints and sinners. Some people are like this, others are like that; some will have healthy bodies, others will have bodies that are unhealthy, from inception. Some will have healthy brains; others will have unhealthy brains. And some of these poor suckers will end up in an asylum or jail because their brains are funny. So they act funny in the world and that's the way it is. After all, it is only a thin line of genes, chemicals and chemical reactions that divides the so-called "normal" behavior from the "abnormal."[1] We see a similar thing happening in those suffering from schizophrenia and Alzheimer's Disease, who because of chemical imbalances in the brain are also acting "funny."

CF: So you wouldn't try to make changes if given the opportunity?

RP: Well, to a certain extent, changes will occur naturally as a result of one's very being and not so much through a conscious intention or will to change. But you should also not be intentionally passive and say "I am a fatalist." Knowing and understanding that one is not the "doer" does not mean one should intentionally abstain from action. Whatever happens in this respect, the "doing" will go on; however you look upon yourself, as a "doer" or "non-doer," that does not make any difference.

You should educate children to the best of your abil-

1 A few months after this interview took place, the *Los Angeles Times* (October 22, 1993) published an article entitled "Researchers Link Gene to Aggression" by its medical writer, Sheryl Stolberg, which starts as follows:

"More than three decades ago, a Dutch schoolteacher, troubled by a pattern of violence among his male relatives, traced the pattern's origin to a couple who married in 1780. He concluded that his kin must be suffering from an inherited mental disability. Pretending to be a dispassionate outsider, he wrote up his notes under the title 'A Curious Case.' The teacher has long since died. But today, his 'curious case' earns a page in the annals of science as a team of researchers from the Netherlands and the United States reports that some men in his family harbor a mutant gene that predisposes them to aggressive behavior." The article continues:

"The discovery of what has been dubbed the 'aggression gene' . . . adds to a growing body of evidence that indicates biological factors, as well as social and environmental causes, contribute to violent behavior.

Researchers were led to an enzyme called monoamine oxidase A, a brain chemical that helps break down several neurotransmitters that — if permitted to build up — might cause a person to overreact to stress. Urine samples taken from from three affected men showed they lacked this crucial enzyme . . . but the enzyme was present in the urine of men who were not affected."

ity and bring them up in the right way, as parents and as educators, naturally. You should have good schools and decent living conditions for all, which more often than not are completely lacking in our society. The opportunities provided should be equal for all. But beyond that, you essentially can't change the fact that things are unequal. That's the crux of the matter: things are unequal. Equality is an ideal that we have cooked up, the notion that we should all be the same. It is not possible, nor even desirable.

CF: Why not desirable?

RP: Because it is against nature, the nature of things. In nature there is and must be movement; it is never static. And in the very movement there will be the higher and the lower, the better and the worse. You have to accept that things are the way they are. We have a concept of a perfect world. But it is only a concept! Accept the reality, things as they are. This is the first thing to do. If you are interested in spirituality, you must accept yourself the way you are and try to find out what's behind all this, what lies at the bottom of it. Is this phenomenon that I watch which I call the "world" and that which I call "my personality," are they all there is? And that personality is born, it develops, and it dies — all for nothing? So what am I doing in this world? What is it all about? All this fuss, and why should I fuss? Why should I make myself busy, acquiring things, trying to survive, and all that business? You come to that position of questioning and weighing things eventually, when you become introspective in the most serious way.

CF: So there is a recognition of not being the "doer," which is what our society is based upon?

RP: Not being the doer, that is right. But, you see, most of us never question our assumptions. We assume so many things, and all these things are from hearsay. As Maharaj said, "Go back to the state you were in before you were born." You have no actual experience of that, the birth; you assume that you were born, because everybody talks in this way. "You were born." So, I just repeat: "I am born." But I have not been present at my birth, I have not seen it, I don't know. As far as I am concerned, I have always been here. I have been something, or more accurately: I have always been. That "I" has always been there, and I don't know anything about my death either. I don't think I will be conscious of the actual dying as "event"; one moment I will be conscious and the next moment I will have lost the consciousness, just as in going to sleep.

CF: How do you equate that with memory, Robert? That just because there wasn't an awareness of your birth, that it simply isn't a lapse of memory or a suppressed memory?

RP: What is the case when you are soundly asleep? Is your memory operating when you are dreamlessly asleep? No, and yet you exist. So if it were a question of memory only, that you create your Beingness with memory, then you should not even be there. When you receive a blow on the head and are knocked out, or when you are fainting, then memory is just a superstructure, a superimposition on your Being. So memory can never be the criterion or *sine qua non* for Being, or the emergence of Being (what you call "birth").

And in deep meditation you will see, as you engage in it, that the thoughts slow down — the thoughts that are created from memory, because without memory there is no thought. And the emotions and feelings, in turn, arise from thought, because without thought there can be no feeling, no emotion. If all that subsides, then you are in what is called an Emptiness, yet there is a Fullness because you exist. And you have peace at that moment, and all that activity as a child . . . .

CF: Could you say that is real memory?

RP: Memory may be actual, but it is never real. Memory is a reaction; it's an impulse from the engrams in the brain cells, what we call "the past." Thus, the past being only the content of memory, it has no reality. Further, if the past does not exist then the future, being a projection from the past, can have no reality either. So with neither the past nor the future being real, time does not exist. Whatever exists only is a timeless moment, beyond space-time; it is Presence itself.

CF: I had a chance to work with the word "remember,"

because it was bugging me and exploring it in the sense of Sanskrit and Greek. And what I came up with as a working definition is that remembering means to participate fully in something. And how I chose to look at that was: What is my being, living in the moment, what is it participating in?

RP: When you are fully participating, there is no memory. Surely, because if you have memory, you can't be fully into something. Because memory will bring about other memories, and then you are constantly in the past, the process of conceptualization. It is a reaction to an experience. And rather than your being participating in everything, everything is really participating in "you," as the Totality.

CF: So memory is always secondary at best, never primary in that sense?

RP: Yes, that is correct. When you love somebody, or you love something, memory does not enter into it. You just love; there is no rationale. When you engage in some activity with love, you don't need any justification. You don't need to bring up past experiences; you just love what you are doing. So it is a form of Being, your natural Being. But memory makes you doubt, makes you slide into conflict. It brings into being the process of time. The memory is time; it is always based on the past. As I said earlier, we are all doing time because we have that as a process of memory.

CF: We never examine the types of assumptions we make all the time.

RP: We must become aware of our faulty way of functioning. And when you become aware of it, then something happens. You see that you are not in tune with yourself, that there is something that is being arrested; in Zen they call it the "stopping of the mind." It is this automaton that we are, this mechanical operation, which is being exposed at that point and comes to an end. Then the momentary blockage is removed and you are restored to the natural flow of life.

CF: One must have faith in that as well, in the true sense of an "inseeing."

RP: Faith is not needed because it is happening, you are experiencing it, the spontaneity. Then you know what you are, you are a process. You are not this entity, with all these memories. You are something far beyond. And you are that in various conditions including the state of being blissfully asleep; then there is this great happiness. And when you wake up in the morning, you can testify: "I slept wonderfully and felt wonderful," because you were free from all this mentation, all this duality which is conflict — potentially or actually. In deep sleep there is no conflict. And the beauty is that you get an inkling of your natural state through that deep sleep state. The last thing before falling asleep, it is very useful to go into oneself, to relax, and watch. Let the mind quieten by itself. And again, be aware first thing in the morning on waking, when you are not yet fully awake and no longer fully asleep and you don't know who you are (that is, the various concepts have not arisen yet.) Wakefulness has come and sleep has gone; at that moment, you are totally free. Do this and you will become more and more aware and free in these moments, before all the superimpositions of consciousness have descended upon your real nature. That is very useful; it gives you a foretaste of the full state of spiritual freedom, when you are no longer "doing time"!

CF: There is some talk these days of the "crazy wisdom" tradition, which as a thread seems to run through all the great traditions.

RP: You mean like Da Free John and others?

CF: I think people would say he represents some of that; some of the greatest teachers who on the surface seem to be the most immoral. Could you speak a little on that?

RP: Well, I think that, from the conventional point of view, these teachers and teachings — even our discussion right here — must seem quite crazy to an outsider because there is a complete flouting of the accepted assumptions and conceptions. When you pick things to pieces as you do, through investigation, through meditation, and you unravel the conventional world view until it is all gone and it is all seen to be part of one's conditioning, then, of course, to the conventionally conditioned person, it is totally crazy what is going on. Because all values are turned upside down, and so there is an aspect of spirituality that is apparently utter madness. When this kind of craziness impacts on the ordinary, conditioned consciousness, it may occasionally shock a very few people into recognition of the Otherness, something deeper than mere conditioned living, resulting in an inward turning. This is well exemplified in various religious expressions. For instance, you have the "crazy Buddhist monk" and in Sufism, you have Mulla Nasrudin, the irrepressible jester and free spirit, who represents the complete outsider.

It is rather odd when you first go through this process of waking up to your real self: you act crazy, you feel like a simpleton and outsider within the established order; there is a distinct feeling of not fitting in. You see that the societal values don't apply to your being, but you have not yet got the understanding to have sympathy for the receptivity of the average person, so your behavior does not take into consideration the limitations of your fellow beings when you start acting so unconventionally.

CF: So your behavior becomes highly random?

RP: Right, but only as it appears to others.

CF: So you are not showing compassion for the person you are in relationship with?

RP: Right, that's at the beginning of the freeing process.

As Maharaj emphasizes all the time, this understanding is initially not sufficient in itself and has to mature and develop fully. As he further states, initially certain persons may also seem unduly occupied with themselves, but that is nothing to worry about as it is a passing phase. Then later, one starts taking into account the point of view of the average person and understands more fully how one impacts on him. And then you make allowances for this, and you mellow out, as it were. So there is this passing through a period of craziness or crazy wisdom.

CF: So it is a phase, it is not a complete maturity that one passes through.

RP: It is not a complete maturity, as I indicated. Of course, ultimately, to the average person, the spiritual person, what he does and how he behaves, will always be seen as a kind of craziness because it is beyond him.

CF: For they are living in different worlds.

RP: They are living in fundamentally different worlds. What we can't understand, we are apt to designate as "crazy," or as "immoral," or whatever.

CF: My teacher has always stated the position that however spontaneous the outlandish behavior might be, for example, the seduction of students that we see going on so much today, if it results in pushing away one spiritual aspirant from the genuine spiritual path, then that would not be worthwhile. Do you agree?

RP: Yes. You see, what has been going on recently with certain masters could almost be foreseen. The relationship between the sexes is quite natural and part of our being in a body. So one should not expect any physical activity in this area necessarily to be different or stop with one who is spiritually inclined or developed. But lying and cheating is another matter, because that implies there still is an ego center. (Naturally, I am not talking here of that exceptional case of lying for the sake of a greater good.) If you love the Self, then you love the Truth. Why should a master resort to duplicity? These are inconsistencies that cannot be glossed over.

CF: So listen to the message and forget the messenger?

RP: The message always comes first and foremost. The messenger is there for the message. You may love your master, but you will still miss if you do not embrace his teaching wholeheartedly. That is why I said in the beginning, when you asked me, that I didn't regret too much the fact of not having seen Maharaj. Since I was primarily interested in *advaita*, I was naturally interested in his approach, but I benefited no less from that of Sri Ramana Maharshi, Sri Krishna Menon and others. You might say, my interest in the matter was all-embracing and non-exclusive. The master is only a help, a signpost. After he has given you something, the essential instructions to get started, then let him go. Then you must stand on your own feet; otherwise there is the danger of continuous dependence.

CF: The inner guru must be turned to?

RP: The inner guru is ever there. Who is the live master's inner guru? He is the same as your own inner guru. The external guru is only a physical manifestation of the sole inner guru. So, the best way to serve your master is by honoring your own inner guru. The guru is actually my Self; it is an idea we have that they are separate.

CF: So when we see these teachers putting on certain affectations, they are possibly forgetting this fact that it is the inner guru that communicates and does the work with the student, not the personality.

Would you comment on how you came to be drawn to *advaita*?

RP: Oh, I can't really explain. It just happened. I don't think one seeks it out; it seeks one out, rather. You stumble upon it and recognize the truth that has always been with you. Certain hints you get; it could be through reading, through talking to people. It might also be none of the above, it could simply be a spontaneous re-cognition of what you are and have always known on some level of your being. As a child, you have known it and you then functioned in a non-dual way; but when you grew older, you were fooled by societal pressures and the truth got drowned out. You were intimidated and lost something precious. So it is not so much a matter of how you come to it, how you have searched it out, because it was always there, deep within you. But it has been suppressed or was overwhelmed by personal and societal pressures, which basically come to the same thing, and you get lost. Then there are perhaps moments of deep conflict or crisis you experience; you go to the root causes of the conflict and, in doing so, recognize the original purity you had as a child. And then you throw away the whole superstructure that you had imbibed from the world around you, and you become your true self once again. You recognize yourself in the act and you hold on to that. It is not a matter of creating something new; it is a re-cognition, and a re-centering. And then it is a natural thing; after all, even the term "non-duality" or *advaita* can easily become a concept on its own, when in fact, it is meant to be the end of all concepts. But unless it has actually taken hold of you, it becomes a dry intellectual thing and then it is a concept.

CF: You did mention hanging on to it, once the re-centering and re-cognition had occurred.

RP: Well, that's a misleading impression that might imply to an outsider that you are doing something. It is not like that; it is a continual rediscovery, which is different from "hanging on" to something, when it becomes a conscious thing. It is a negative process. You come to non-duality through discarding all duality — the *via negativa*. You cannot directly get to it, grasp it; there is nothing to grasp, an Emptiness. It is the very antithesis of concreteness, something that can't be grasped. It is totally effusive, ethereal. And yet it is what everything else is based upon — rock bottom. Maharaj calls it that, too: that Emptiness is hard as rock. It is the real, and everything else becomes soft like butter and dreamlike. All so-called concrete things in this world that we take as solid are only wisps of ideas, figments of one's imagination. So if you start grasping for it, it will ever elude you. You must naturally fall into it. See that all this world of concept is false and the real will be there, but don't try to find the real in any other way. Always approach the real through seeing the false.

CF: Are you making those distinctions and continuing to refine the distinctions more and more — the false and the real?

RP: They are not a pair of opposites.

CF: So once the false has been recognized, the real will appear.

RP: You can see the false through the real, because there is only the real; that lies at the bottom of everything. Even the false has some of the real in it, because it emerges from the real. And ultimately, there is only the real; the false or *Maya* does not actually exist because it is brought forth by our imperfect way of seeing "things," just like the snake in the rope never really existed.

CF: To change the subject a little bit, would you say that sacred art springs from the recognition of the Emptiness? And a lot of art is an attempt to get to the real?

RP: Not so much an attempt as a natural outflowing from the state of Being. It is the greatest art that functions from that. It is art itself and then whatever you do is art.

CF: My secondary question in there is that there is a lot of art that springs from the false.

RP: Yes, that is intellectual art. Everything is sacred when it comes from the source. Then your whole being is sacred. But as long as you are ignorant about yourself, you can't even talk about sacredness. Then there is no sacredness; it is all starting from illusion and expressing itself as illusion.

CF: Do you agree with the Hindu teaching that the world is a dream state?

RP: Yes. *Maya.*

CF: So, if one is awake, whatever occurs in *Maya* is not of any concern?

RP: That goes back to what we were discussing earlier about making attempts to improve the world.

CF: In Maharaj's later years, did he ever mention that he was hopeful about his message reaching the West?

RP: Yes. He actually preferred the foreigners to the Indians for his students, because he felt that the foreigners understood better than his own people, they had more open minds and less vested interests, were held back less through the burden of tradition.

CF: It is interesting because Germany has just really opened up to spiritual teachings.

RP: There were people who went to Maharaj simply as a routine as it were, because they were underprivileged, as most of the people of India are. But these were very poor, even by Indian standards, who could hardly make it through the day. And at Maharaj's they were given some food after the *prasad* (an offering to the guru by bestowing food through this Indian ritual). These people were visiting regularly and enjoying social support from the group. And Maharaj made the comment once that some of these people would have died long ago had they not found this support.

CF: So he didn't seem to mind that. For whatever reason someone came to his talks, that was O.K.

RP: Yes, but he did mind people who were trying to get into an argument with him just to show off their erudition. Also, he was less welcoming to those who came out of sheer curiosity. He would ask them to leave in no uncertain terms.

CF: I read where he was criticized for clinging to ritual, and he said that was fine, that the rituals were started at one time and it seemed to support people in this process, like singing the *bhajans* (holy songs).

RP: It seemed to create a receptivity — a certain mood, and the mind quiets and is bothering you less, it lowers its interference. You know that — changing the subject a little — Ramana Maharshi said that when you are in that state of freedom, it is like being in a state of dreamless sleep while awake — a combination of the two conditions. Do you follow?

CF: Yes. I am a one-time practitioner of TM, involved with the idea of witnessing the various states of consciousness.

RP: What Maharshi was referring to is a state of functioning normally, that is, having the everyday reactions in which you relate to people and do your job and all those things, but where at the same time that feverish activity of the mind — imagining things, fear and emotions — has subsided to such an extent that you become as if being in the state of sleep. I don't know whether you have experienced this. I know it's possible to be fully asleep and yet be aware. Then the dream of the sleep and the waking state are coming closer together.

CF: In TM that is referred to as restful alertness, or witnessing in sleep. And in terms of stages of consciousness, the Hindus call it *turya*, the fourth state after waking, dreaming and sleep.

RP: So, how are you going to present all this?

CF: I have no idea. [*laughter*]

RP: You know, the truth of all we have talked about is ever available. It is lying in wait for us and has infinite patience. So that when your defenses are down, and you are tired of this superficial, worldly life without meaning and you begin to see the impossibility of ever coming out winning through such a process, then there is a possibility of genuine spiritual awakening. And by "winning," I mean becoming stabilized, centered on all levels. Even if you gained all the riches and fame of the world, you would still not be internally at rest, centered, stabilized, and you would be missing out on the bliss which is available anytime and anyplace and is a natural prerogative of any conscious being. The bliss that immeasurably outweighs any gratification available through the usual worldly life . . . .

Once you come to that crucial point of exhaustion with the worldly process, then you are highly susceptible to letting the truth enter into your heart. It is not just a matter of the intellect; it is all your faculties, the emotions, your total being. That is why Ramana Maharshi calls your real self the Heart. When you discover yourself for what you are, that you have been living a lie by thinking you were something entirely different, then everything happens by itself and you see the lie as the prison. But you must discover the lie first. In this process, for most of us, there must be a teacher of sorts. That presence of the teacher may be just for a few seconds. There is a story that some spiritual aspirant was sitting in a courtyard and a page from the Upanishads was blown about by the wind. And as the man was sitting there, that one page from the sacred writings fell right at his feet; he picked it up and read a few lines. And that was enough; that was his teacher, that moment became the decisive turning point in his life.

CF: So the spontaneous teacher could be a rock; it could literally be anything?

RP: Yes, that is correct. What and how this happens depends once again on one's *prarabdha*. Zen is full of examples of that. But it must be an awakening as to one's present state of sleep. We are lost! [*chuckle*] Suddenly, you see something . . . that all I have been doing is just a waste of time; that is really what it amounts to. And now I know I don't have to do a thing because I see what *is* and I see what I am, and I let things happen from there.

CF: And I must live with that.

RP: Live with that, but it happens! You don't "do" anymore.

CF: You come to disassociate from "doing" at that point, when the recognition is there.

RP: The recognition is there and the doing has stopped. Because whatever "doing" you do, it is going back, sliding back into your old habits. Habitual doing in order to gain this, gain that, become respectable, become wealthy, even trying to become "wise" — it is all the height of foolishness.

CF: I think that the fear that arises in people when they hear this type of talk is that this is a real isolationist point of view.

RP: And, in essence, it is the very opposite. No isolationism is possible. Because when you see yourself without boundaries, how can that be isolationism? It is the other way around: It is those in society that live dualistically who live behind walls all the time; in the deeper sense, they are the true isolationists. Each of them lives as a separate being, an "I." And so we have wars and friction between classes, nations, people of different colors, etc. People seem to be judged by their physical characteristics . . . males and females . . . with their respective liberation movements . . . all this nonsense that is going!

CF: Are you also referring to the men's liberation movement?

RP: It is total madness!

CF: It seems a lot of denial is going on with people in society today, people denying parts of themselves. Can you address that a little bit?

RP: Yes, the denial is there because it is enforced from the outside. If you are told to be such and such, you have an idea in mind, you must live up to that ideal of, say, a middle-class, well-to-do person, or that of a well-educated, working-class person — especially in England, with the class distinctions still being very strong there, but you have them in India too, with the different castes, where each person has to behave accordingly — you will have that reluctance to let go and be your natural self. Your behavior is entirely governed by what society dictates. So you are not really yourself; the most essential part of your being you constantly deny, because you live only with the superstructure — what you are supposed to be and how you are supposed to behave. Nor are those who superficially rebel against the existing order of things any different, because they, in turn, rigidly conform to their own code of rebellion. All this, of course, means the death of spontaneity and intuitive functioning.

CF: And we are always trying to measure up to something we can never attain.

RP: Never. How can you? Because these are ideas; there is always more . . . . If you are good, then you will have to be better. If you are "moral," you have to become more moral, more virtuous, but what is "virtue"? That is society's concept.

CF: I see a real insidiousness in this when it is discovered that the higher one gets the more sensitive one becomes to a fall. So you are actually constantly becoming more vulnerable to those negative aspects the more you are achieving and the more you are growing in that direction. You are sensitive to failure . . .

RP: So society thinks it is O.K. to lock people up, to separate them from society. I also see that as a necessity. But I am very much against the idea of locking them up because you feel you have to take vengeance or punish them. It is none of our business. Whose business is it other than that of the creator of this world?

CF: Yes. So should anyone be playing God, as we always take it upon ourselves?

RP: Now, our society looks upon criminals almost as a different race and "bad." I look upon them as unfortunate souls and their condition as an illness or a deficiency. They need some treatment, and, in most cases, they can be treated; but if not, if they are too mentally ill, then you have to keep them in a place where they can't do any further harm — maybe for the rest of their lives. It is only common sense; you want to protect the community. If you know a hurricane is coming, you try to keep out of harm's way; you take reasonable precautions so that the damage is minimized. You do the same thing with a dangerous criminal. You put him in a place where he can do no further harm. But you don't go to him and say "I am going to punish you, knock you on the head, because you are bad." Who am I to say so?

CF: So a contextual shift is needed in the way we view criminals. They have to be seen more as patients in a hospital in terms of mores than an actual "bad" person that will never change or has no opportunity.

RP: Yes. The thing is that if the individual concerned realizes that society treats him appropriately, his attitude will also get less bitter and then there is some prospect of his rehabilitation. After all, he is also part of humanity and part of consciousness. And to brutalize him further does not help. And yet, that is what we are doing now. The energy we are currently spending on this problem is lost, as far as I am concerned.

We should just prevent these people from doing any further harm, and see if there is a chance that they can regenerate themselves. In this connection, the Prison Library Project may play a part by educating prisoners, not only intellectually but also spiritually. There is so much opportunity for them; they have the time and maybe also, in some cases, the inclination for going into themselves and discovering how they got into this whole process of crime in the first place. But when you treat somebody like dirt, that person will act like dirt. If you treat him with dignity, he is more likely to respond in kind. Oppression creates only more oppression and bitterness. So the prison system should become a meditational system as much as possible. But limited resources are, of course, a big problem. But this does not mean that the Prison Library Project necessarily needs tremendous resources.

CF: One last question. One part we didn't tape was the discussion of the *bhajans* and the setting of mood as being almost a soil for transformation, as you put it.

RP: Yes, there must be a quiet mind first. If you are talking to me in an effort to teach me something, and I am all the time thinking of something else that I have to do the next moment, I can't pay attention to you. So if I am restless or nervous about something, I can't give proper attention. I must give total attention, in these matters in particular. You can't deal with this with only a part of your mind. Nowadays, we do so many things — we eat and watch television and try to carry on a conversation — all at the same time.

But with this thing, you can't do that. First of all, you have to be very quiet within yourself, so that you are open. If you are busy in your mind, or even if you hold something back, you are not all there to be part of this interchange. The interchange between a teacher and a disciple is a unique process. It is almost a blending of two individuals — that process of finding out what is the basis of all our thought, all our emotion. You have to be totally open; otherwise you cannot discover this. So it is important to be in that absolutely receptive mood, and that receptivity can only come when there is a deep silence. And the *bhajans* create, or help create, that state of seriousness and dedication to the Ultimate. Then reality can be imparted.

If you can be truly silent here and now, then you may not need the *bhajans*. In that case, you don't need anything; you are just silence itself. But most people who are beginning to discover this thing, they have no silence within. The interior silence may come at the end of the process, as it were; they can't begin with it, when they need it most. Therefore, anything that creates a restful, peaceful atmosphere will be a help.

CF: Thank you, Robert.

12

CONVERSATION WITH SRI POONJA

In March of 1993, I had the privilege of spending a week with Sri Poonja in Lucknow, India. Poonjaji has recently become known in the West, mainly through a book he published under the title *Wake Up and Roar (Volumes 1 and 2)* and some interviews he gave to American journalists that were published in such periodicals as the *Yoga Journal* (Sept./Oct. 1992) and *The Inquiring Mind* (Fall 1992).

The following are a few biographical details. Sri Poonja was born on October 13, 1910, in the western part of the Punjab. He experienced his first *samadhi* (state of bliss) at the age of nine. In 1944, he met his master, Sri Ramana Maharshi. Like that other great Indian teacher, Sri Nisargadatta Maharaj, Poonjaji was a householder. Much of his working life was spent in the field as a mining inspector. Until his death in 1997, he resided in Lucknow, where hundreds of people from all over the world sought his spiritual council, and a few of his pupils are now spreading his message in the West.

The main virtue of his teaching, as I see it, is its universality and simplicity. It does not require any prior theoretical knowledge on the part of the student, and is reminiscent of the direct transmission as practiced in Zen. In fact, Poonjaji himself states he has nothing to teach, and there is no teaching. All that is required from the student is to let the mind fall silent. Our constant thought activity leads only to misery (*samsara*). A still mind, on the other hand, is man's greatest blessing. It opens us up to bliss (*ananda*), which is not conditional upon external circumstances. Everything will be revealed in that state and *only* in that state. This, much simplified, seems to me the essence of his "non-teaching."

While in Lucknow, I had the opportunity to discuss with him a problem that had engaged me for some time, and that resulted from statements made by J. Krishnamurti and his namesake U.G. Krishnamurti on the subject of body-mind interaction, especially as it relates to the enlightenment process. The following is a verbatim report of our interchange:

RP: My question is about the relationship, if any, between the psyche and the soma. According to J. Krishnamurti, at the moment of liberation, there is also a physical transformation of the brain cells. Is this correct or incorrect, or are in a way perhaps both correct and incorrect? Another thinker, U.G. Krishnamurti, relates that psychological transformation is wholly a bodily process and cannot be affected in any way by one's mode of perceiving reality. I seem to have discerned the proper answer to these questions the other day when you said that in real freedom there is no longer even the mind, thoughts and the body. So all these points of view have dropped away as unnecessary and irrelevant conceptualizations. Am I understanding you correctly?

Poonjaji: To speak of any cells in the body, brain cells, is merely a physical idea, because the cells are in the brain; so it belongs to physicality.

As to the other question, U. G. says he does not agree. So both these concepts are not correct in my view. Because whether you agree or disagree, they belong to the same mind. They come from the mind. So the total freedom, ultimate reality, is that never ever anything existed. So who is to understand if there are body cells or not? Who is to say to be against or in favor? To say something in favor, you need mind. What is mind itself? You don't need any mind. You never existed. Nothing ever existed. Not even the creator itself. And we all belong to the creator . . . . (But) when you speak of creation, there must have been a creator. I don't think a creator had been created before any creation. Before creation there must have been something, which cannot be spoken of or described. You can't give it a name of even Nothingness, Emptiness, Enlightenment, Freedom or whatever. There is no word (for it) . . . . Word is only a definition of communication between two persons . . . . Nothing but God was there; that is God, ultimate reality and that is always there, here and now. Not that you have to gain or attain it through some teacher. You have to return to your ultimate understanding: Where does this concept come from that I exist? "I exist." . . . if you search for the source of "I," it will straightway takes you to this place or no-place I just spoke about.

Further Comments by RP: Poonjaji's statement reverberates with that of Zen Master Hui-neng's famous pronouncement: "From the first, not a thing is."

Even on the level of physicality, the comments of both Krishnamurtis are a moot point, since the one-to-one relationship between mind and one particular body — which forms the basis of that "one" who has a particular body, makes statements about "me" and "mine," and also about that particular body's cells — is seen to be invalidated. You see, to talk about "body" implies a question of exclusivity — "body" being synonymous with boundaries — and the unspoken question in the background remains: "Whose?" Whose body are we talking about? To tie any particular body to a particular entity or "I" is the basis of all ignorance and the foundation stone of duality. In other words, seen from the point of view of *advaita* (non-duality), to talk about "my body" or "somebody" immediately opens up a can of worms.

Then when that level is further transcended, in going from consciousness to Awareness — the ultimate background to experience — there is no longer even mind or body. For body rests on mind, as Poonjaji once said "Body is only a thought." Then what is talked about as "body" is a concept and definition by "mind" — and mind, in turn, is only an abstraction, a fixation through memory in the stream of time, and otherwise nonexistent. Can you show me your mind? Time, in turn, is nothing but a stream of thoughts, and can only be seen as actually existing through memory, as a projection. So, in effect, mind is time, and time is mind. Both are figures of speech. When time is seen for what it is, what is left only is the Present — not as an intersection between the future and the past, but as pure "isness," or as it is called in Zen, "suchness." That "suchness" is totally alien to the concept of time; in fact, it is timeless or true Eternity. In that isness, there is not the slightest trace of mind, body or thought, and so to talk about what Nisargadatta would call "grossified forms," such as cells and their biological mutations, is no longer relevant.

13

WHERE IS THE SELF? WHERE IS "I"-NESS?

What all living beings have in common is experience, and it is this, obviously, that one has to study in the first place. By experience we mean some sort of reactivity to the environment, from the simple reaction of an unicellular organism like the amoeba to the five sense organs and highly developed cortex of *Homo sapiens.*

Let us as an example consider the mechanism of vision. The eyes see a shape that is recognized (i.e., resembling previous impressions, associated with the semantic engram of the term "house"), this sensory information is processed by the optical nerve and passed on to the brain, resulting in the percipient's observation: "I see a house," or "there stands a house."

The question that now must be faced is: Is there indeed an objective reality of a "house," a "real house"? The mind says it sees a "house," but it is a "consciousness house." Reflected light is collected and focused by the lens of the eye, resulting in an inverted image on the retina. Specialized cells behind the retina convert this image into nerve impulses that travel down the optical nerve to the vision center of the brain. At this point, the image of the house no longer exists; there are only electrical impulses, coded information moving along neurons. The image of the house must be re-created in the visual center.

Now I maintain there is no real house at all at any time — existent independent from my brain, or from anybody's brain, for that matter. Naturally, the same applies for any observation made by the sense-organ/brain system. The implications of this perceived mechanism are profound and radically upsetting to the established way of thinking. First of all, it challenges the traditional view that our existence is primarily physical in nature, and that our fate rests on and is tied up entirely with the body.

As we follow the pathway of perception, it will be seen that a purely physical process — a linear chain of events — progresses, in which there is no perceiver nor a perceived. It is much like a series of billiard balls passing along an initial impact from the very first ball. Thus the initial stimulation of the sense organs — which may be light, heat, sound, pressure, taste — is transmitted to the brain. At this end station, the great mystery occurs: there is realization of a perception having taken place: "I see a house," or I hear a sound, I feel cold, pressure, etc. And at this brain end-station, the physical movement is transformed into a mental experience or what we call "perception." At this point, consciousness expresses itself, there is mention of an object having been perceived, but at no point is there a subject, an experiencer, or perceiver involved. Only the limitation of language forces us into believing this: I saw a house, instead of "a house appeared in consciousness," etc. For the same reason, one is not allowed to say it appeared in *my* consciousness, because there is no evidence that that consciousness has any limitations or divisions. Thus, one is not allowed to say *my* consciousness or *your* consciousness, because that demarcation is based on the body, and the body itself is observed within consciousness and is therefore secondary to it. From this inquiry, it follows that the only real Subject is the Consciousness or the "I-I," as the Maharshi used to call it. Like the tenth man in the famous story, it is ever overlooked, yet is always there.

A few further pertinent observations may be made here. First, the linear process described appears to be in time. A finite distance for the impulse needs to be traversed, so passage of time is obviously involved, however small the amount may be. At the end of this process, a qualitatively different event takes place: the perception arises of a particular object or sensory impression in the manner described, and this latter event appears to arise spontaneously and immediately, without being processed in time. First, there is a silent process, as it were; then all of a sudden, the perception makes itself felt in a conspicuous manner — that is, consciously and timelessly. Where is the Self? Where is "I-ness"? There is nothing identifiable as such. Thus, the statement "I see a house, hear a sound," etc. is incorrect and must be rectified. It should be amended to "there is a house," "there is a sound," or whatever the case may be. As Ramana Maharshi and Nisargadatta admonished us: Upon investigation of the question: Who am I?, it will be found that there is actually no self or "I" at all! What exists only is the consciousness, and what we call "objects" are only mental constructions assembled from sensory impressions. These mental constructions have no reality of their own, that is, apart from the consciousness. The world is within you, sensations are within you, space and time are within you. You are the infinite source of all.

14

Realization of Self through Short-Circuiting the Thought Process

We have only two choices: We are either spirit or we are not. If you realize your spirit nature, there is no further argument. If you see yourself as a physical being, existing in a space-time dimension, a material entity, separate from other "things," the following will prove that you are not. For example, a man is looking at a tree. There is a source of light, the sun. Then, as discussed in our previous meeting, light from the sun is reflected by the tree, picked up and focused by the lens of the eye, to make an inverted image on the back of the retina. Science tells us that specialized sensory cells behind the retina convert this inverted image into nerve impulses that travel down the optic nerve. These impulses eventually make their way to the visual center at the back of the head. It is important to note that the image of the tree no longer exists at this point. Only electrical impulses, coded information moving along neurons. The image of the tree must be recreated in the visual center; i.e., brought into visual consciousness. The tree you see is not the real tree, it is actually a mental reconstruction projected by the mind. Look around and realize that everything is mind. All is a facsimile, produced in consciousness. Nothing is real. This then is the leap into spirit. Nothing is physical or material. Awareness and spirit are one and this is our identity.

Very well put. I would like, however, to address one important point. When stating that our ultimate identity is "spiritual," this might be misunderstood by some. The word "spiritual" may be equated with "mental." "Mental" is the field of the mind, and mind is still very much bound up with the body. There we are still firmly in the realm of duality. For example, when pain registers through the mind, there is no doubt about which part of the body is affected. Awakening into *advaita* is clearly beyond all physicality, as was well brought out by Poonjaji in my discussion with him about the nature of brain cells. In the transcended state, there is neither body, mind nor even spirit as commonly understood. And although pain is still present, there is no longer any identification, whether physically or psychologically, with the pain.

Let us now have a closer look at the issues you raised. Is anything truly "Real"?

To properly understand our real constitution and situation in the general scheme of things, it may be helpful — at least initially — to visualize our psychosomatic makeup as a sensory-perceptive container. This container represents the field of operation of the five organs of sense perception — sight, hearing, feeling, tasting and smelling. That there are no fewer or more than five need not be of concern, nor is it possible to envisage others because our scope for projection of hypothetical sense organs is circumscribed by these very same existent senses. Our imagination is woven from the texture of the existing sensory perceptive fields and is inherently restricted to that structure. In other words, it is impossible to think on the matter by extrapolation from our existent condition because such thinking would still be based upon perception through the very same five sense organs. We are boxed, in as it were, by our existent constitution!

In proceeding with the investigation, I want to focus on the sense of sight, though one might equally well zero in on any of the other sensory perceptions. Thus, what is being said about visual perception is merely by way of example and applies similarly to all other forms of perception. In the waking state, one is aware of the world. The eyes perceive an "object." I won't define it any further, saying, for example: "I see a tree," because this would be like jumping the gun and introducing an unwarranted extrapolation, the process of naming and recognition. But above all, it would solidify illusion, such as giving the impression that there actually exists a "real tree" or a real anything at all somewhere. In exploring the possibility of there being a "real world," I have to discover if anything actually exists apart from myself. The obvious alternative to this is that I have created this apparent world myself. And this is, in fact, what becomes revealed if I go into it: *There is no real tree, no real anything at all,* and that the tree or whatever has only semantic reality, through the perceiver assigning the concept of "treeness" to a sensory stimulation. Even to say that there is an "object" is on the borderline of the permissible, as what is taking place only is that there is light entering the eye and ultimately, via various physiological intermediate events, registration in the consciousness through pattern recognition accompanied by the formation of language (of which, incidentally, according to Sri Nisargadatta Maharaj, there are four stages).

But does not the same insight of the non-reality of all things apply equally to the very sensory perception box induced above? The entire sequence of light entering the eye, followed by registration and recognition, and ending with the statement of an observer perceiving an object must be questioned. For what this would amount to is explaining or establishing a certain fact in terms that are themselves still to be proved — a flagrant offense against logic. Then it becomes similar to the problem of the chicken and egg, which came first. Thus, we must conclude that the very sense organs of perception are a projection, an invention by the mind and as such pure *Maya.*

What is the meaning of all this? At first glance, this may all seem quite abstract, but in fact we have stumbled upon something quite extraordinary, the discovery of a remarkable and unprecedented closed circuit: The sense organs required to detect the Universe are themselves the creation of the perceiver! Which means the collapse of the entire linear process of sensing, registration in and as consciousness, deduction and induction. This is the demise of the mind. The mental process stops at this very point when it is clear it has come to the end of its tether. Things may appear to happen but I — as the creator and perceiver — have exited from the process and been superseded by "creation"! A creator that has not been created but just *is*.

When one has gone thus far in one's meditation, where is one? One is at once here and now, and nowhere at all — completely divorced from space and time. Because space and time are seen to be secondary projections, wholly conceptual in their nature. "*My* existence" now is extremely nebulous, ethereal almost, whereas what is solid only is "Existence." Furthermore, on the very deepest level, existence and nonexistence are seen to be the same. And anything that I may state as to my condition must be designated as pure fantasy. Silence spontaneously results, which is the only valid statement one can make. The confluence of existence and nonexistence has been called by some the realization of the Void.

At this point, I have completely lost the feeling of being in space and time, because I incorporate the whole of space and time — the infinite past as well as the infinite future. Also, I am the creator of perception/sensation as well as the perceiver/sensor. I am the dreamer of the Universe and, simultaneously, I am the subject of the dream. I am at once the creator of everything and I am everything created, I am the beginning and I am the end — I am my origin and the result of everything created and uncreated — I am the Self, which is nothing and everything.

I found this fresh and utterly unburdened state reflected in the following verses of the *Ribu Gita*[1]:

> The *jivanmukta* is one who possesses the realization: Existing independently of my own self, there is no earth, no five elements, no physical manifestation whatsoever. There is no whole and no part, no oneness and no duality, nothing near or far, high or low, nothing to praise, nothing to be scorned, for I am none other than Brahman.
>
> The *jivanmukta* is one who possesses the firm conviction: For myself in this state, there is neither pleasure nor displeasure, neither delight nor rejoicing, no mistaking of the false for the real, giving rise to duality, nothing to be refuted and nothing to be asserted, no abiding practice of union with the divine, for I am that very Brahman whose nature is Oneness.
>
> The *jivanmukta* is one who dwells in a state beyond all comparison in which he affirms: The colors black, white and red do not exist, neither do the myriad names and forms which men perceive; there is no confusion or clear understanding, nothing which is hidden, and no vast expanse of space, no joy or sorrow, no religious observances. For myself in this state there are no differentiated entities, for I am the all-encompassing supreme Brahman.

1 From the first English translation from the original Indian epic *Sivarahasaya*, translated by Dr. H. Ramamoorthy, assisted by Master Nome. Published by the Society of Abidance in Truth, Santa Cruz, California, USA, 1995.

15

Logic Applies to Thought, Intuition to Consciousness

The last time we met we had a good discussion about sensory input and Consciousness. However, I think we can go even further. You made it clear that sense organs, neurons, etc., which presumably create consciousness, are themselves concepts in Consciousness. Prior to any such concept, consciousness must be present. So when asking whether these "conceptual" sense organs create consciousness or does consciousness manifest the sensory apparatus of eye, neuron, brain, etc., it seems clear that the latter is true. However, there may be a third alternative. If the organs of perception have an independent existence, then both could be true, i.e., sense organs produce consciousness and that same consciousness manifests sense organs as concepts. Because we are contained in this perceptual-conceptual "box," and cannot verify what is outside the box, there must always be some doubt as to our true situation. It seems the answer was already contained in the question. Without considering the possibility of an independent existence of the "world," you ignore the essence of what we seek to discover.

Like the question of which came first, the chicken or the egg, the question excludes the possibility of a third answer. Both the chicken and the egg evolved and changed gradually through time from some ancient pre-chicken ancestor.

Even if the chicken and the egg did evolve from some ancient pre-chicken ancestor, then the question has only been moved back in time to that ancient ancestor. Which came first: the pre-chick or the pre-chick egg? But doesn't all this rather point to a fallacious space-time frame of reference?

But now returning to your main argument, which is that of a third alternative, at the risk of being considered dogmatic, I have to say, first of all, that in no way can the sense organs produce Consciousness. They may appear to be mediating in the process, but by themselves they are totally helpless. It would be the same as saying that your computer all by itself has created a book or work of art. The sense organs are essentially mechanical entities and of a decidedly different order than Consciousness. Sense organs, along with all other objects, are concepts, and in no way ever can concepts give birth to Consciousness — they are in a different dimension of reality. The very concept of "concept" itself requires Consciousness for its existence and expression. One might say that concept is an expression, a modulation of the Consciousness, just as the waves in the ocean are a manifestation of the ocean but have no independent existence apart from it. In truth, the Consciousness is all that exists; it is therefore your very Self.

All the musings about what is inside and outside the box are only possible through Consciousness. Without it, there is nothing but even the idea of nothingness can arise only in Consciousness. Since Consciousness is before anything, even nothingness is dependent on Consciousness and is a pure concept therein.

What do you mean by the independent existence of the world? There is no world without an observer observing that world. There is no object without a subject designating that object. Does the observer exist in your (dreamless) sleep? No, the world is absent because there is no one to observe it. And in your dream the world is different from the world in the waking state — but both worlds need a dreamer to manifest: The "observer" is the "observed"! That's why to reach the Ultimate, reason alone is not sufficient; only intuition will do.

Apparently, you like logic a lot. So do I. But, unfortunately or fortunately, logic can truly mislead us when misapplied to the realm beyond the subject-object relationship, beyond thought. Logic is a particular way of thinking, a special language, as it were. It applies to the world of multiplicity (duality) only; it is based on the relationship of objects with a subject. Since Consciousness is non-dual, logic cannot touch it. In fact, Consciousness is the only thing that really exists, although it is not a "thing." All "things" are only reflections within it. You may devise various *concepts* of Consciousness and then be entitled to apply logic to those, but your conclusion will not appertain to the non-dual Consciousness.

The fact is that intuition transcends logic; it reaches beyond both subject and object, observer and observed. Logic rules relationships, but since Consciousness is the Self, which is the totality (non-dual) and carries everything within its bosom, where is the question of relationship? How can it be subordinated to logic?

Can we use logic, which is thinking or mind or ego, to communicate insights which, in turn, invalidate the very reality of the egoity that proposes these insights? Without the idea of a separate thinker or "I," there can be no subsequent thoughts. Is it sensible then to deny the "I" by asserting the "I" through so-called logical discourse and argument? There is something wrong here, and the more one thinks about it, the more complicated it becomes. I am, in fact, using a logical argument to discount the use of logical argument!

Logic may not lead to truth but it can lead to the end of untruth.

16

By Force of Habit

Having read so many spiritual texts, which all play down the fear of death, I have still not been able to shake off this fear and reconcile myself to my mortality. What is one to do about it?

Have you ever considered why one favors doing certain things? It seems to me that a major factor is habit. Originally, one may have taken up a certain activity because one's mental and physical constitution meshed perfectly with that activity, say, like having a natural talent for chess. Subsequently, one gets better at it, a momentum develops and one has every reason to immerse oneself in the activity. At this stage, one does it unthinkingly and between that "me" and the activity there exists a continuum, like a smoothly running machine. One is "hooked," as it were! Now let me extrapolate to the business of living in general. As a baby, everything was the same to me, at least psychologically, for the mind was practically a blank. However, gradually there developed discrimination, likes and dislikes and a psychological blueprint, a "personality" was formed. From merely experiencing, I began to like certain experiences and dislike others. But generally, I liked my activities and developed an attachment for living in the body, "I loved Life" as the saying goes, and consequently, I abhorred death. Again, through the development of habit, a most fundamental change took place in me: but this time I became "hooked" on life. So our fear of death is actually, and originally, the result of the habit of living. It is certainly our most powerful habit, upon which all other habits are based. Without it, there would be no fear of death! The only thing that could counter that habit is the experience of deep sleep! And that is not actually an "experience" but rather a state of "non-experience." The bliss of this state we have ignored because its memory is overwhelmed by the many more numerous and stronger impressions of the waking state. In sum, the lust for life, or the greed for experience, equals the fear of death.

Thus, the habit of thinking in this particular manner is literally "lethal" for it is that only which creates the disparate and intrinsically separate categories of "life" and "death" — the ultimate dichotomy. And the one effective way of reversing the process, of "waking up," is to constantly live with the full realization of our habits, be they "good" or "bad," and remember the bliss of sleep, which is not a habit but akin to our original state — the state beyond both life and death — and abide in That.

GLOSSARY

advaita	The teaching of non-duality
ananda	Bliss
bhajans	Sacred, devotional songs
bhakti	Devotion
gunas	The three basic attributes or energetic/material qualities that underlie and operate the world process: *sattva* (purity, clarity, harmony), *rajas* (passion, energy, activity) and *tamas* (inertia, resistance, dullness, torpor); Everything in the universe is said to be made up of the three *gunas* in various proportions
jagrat-sushupti	Wakeful sleep
jivanmukta	an awakened soul; liberated one
jnana	Knowledge; more particularly, spiritual knowledge; wisdom
jnani	Literally, "knower"; realized sage
maya	Illusion
parabrahman	Absolute state
prarabdha	Karmic destiny; the portion of one's karma that is being worked out in, and determining the course of, one's present life
rajasic	Having the qualities of *rajas,* producing restlessness and passion, one of the three *gunas*
sadhaka	Spiritual aspirant; advanced seeker
sadhana	Spiritual practices

samadhi	Bliss; spiritual state of absorption
samsara	Illusory nature of reality; suffering from delusion; cycle of births and deaths
samskaras	Innate tendencies that stem from past-life thoughts, words, and deeds; conditioning that results from earlier actions
satchitananda	Existence-Consciousness-Bliss, said to be the nature of the Ultimate Reality
sattvic	Having the quality of *sattva*: purity, simplicity, harmony; one of the three *gunas*
siddhis	Yogic or supernatural powers
vasanas	Latent tendencies of the soul, similar to *samskaras*
vichara	Self-inquiry

BOOKS OF RELATED INTEREST FROM NAB

PSYCHIC POWERS (A Practical Guide Awaken Your Sixth Sense)—***Melita Denning Osborne Phillips***

This practical guide offers complete step-by-step instructions on developing your innate psychic skills in divination, dowsing, clairvoyance, psychometry, and spirit communication. You will learn how to safely enhance your mental and psychic abilities, and to use your abilities to positively change your life and the lives of those around you.

ISBN: 81-7822-051-2

HOW TO MASTER CHANGE IN YOUR LIFE (Sixty-Seven Ways to Handle Life's Toughest Moments)—***Mary Carroll Moore***

This book offers sixty-seven powerful techniques to embrace each challenge with courage, love, and grace. It shows you how to not only cope with change but master it. You can actually use change to achieve personal goals and make your life more spiritually fulfilling.

ISBN: 81-7822-036-9

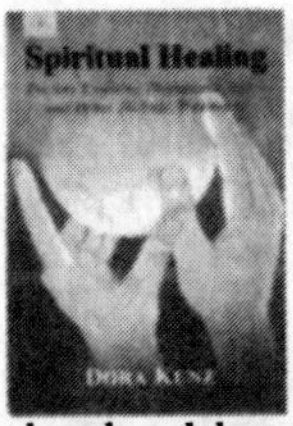

SPIRITUAL HEALING (Doctors Examine Therapeutic Touch and other Holistic treatments)—***Dora Kunz***

Healing is a divine art. The book presents a surprising open-mindedness and forward looking vision. A spiritual revolution is underway in health care. More and more doctors, nurses, and counselors are recognizing that health means treating the soul and the psyche as well as the body.

ISBN: 81-7822-011-3

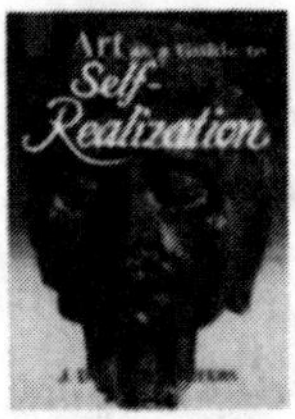

ART AS A GUIDE TO SELF-REALIZATION—***J. Donald Walters***

Art as a Guide to Self-Realization offers a blueprint for the future of art, and shows how art can be a powerful influence for meaningful existence and positive attitudes in society. The book presents a new approach to the arts, one that views both artistic expression and artistic appreciation as creative communication.

ISBN: 81-7822-028-8

THE SELF-REVEALED KNOWLEDGE THAT LIBERATES THE SPIRIT—*Roy Eugene Davis*

In this book the author presents a clear explanation of the soul's awakening through progressive stages of spiritual growth from ordinary, illusional states of awareness to mental illumination, spiritual enlightenment, and liberation of consciousness. The descriptions of philosophical principles will satisfy the rational mind and speak to the heart that aspires to direct perception of truth.

ISBN: 81-7822-050-4

THE INTUITIVE WAY (A Guide To Living From Inner Wisdom)—*Penney Peirce*

It demonstrates practical applications from speeding decision making to expanding personal growth and makes you aware about the following benefits of active intuition: • A positive, life-enhancing attitude • More synchronicity and good luck • Greater efficiency with less effort • Attention to detail while seeing the big picture • Increased creativity and imagination • Confidence in your own insights • Understanding your soul's purpose.

ISBN: 81-7822-008-3

DIALOGUES ON REALITY—*Robert Powell*

Dr. Powell is widely recognized as one of the most inspired writers on the subject of Advaita, the teaching of non-duality. He takes us on a journey beyond the realm of the ego, beyond the illusion of subject and object, good and bad, high and low, to the ground on which the manifest universe rests. This is where the mind and intellect cannot reach and which is beyond words.

ISBN: 81-7822-140-3

PATH WITHOUT FORM— *Robert Powell*

The author invites the reader to accompany him on his own adventures in self-exploration—a journey that spanned several decades and eventually led him to the ultimate teaching of the non-dual nature of reality. It describes the milestones achieved by the author on the path of deliverance with the hope that they may be of some help to others in their own emancipation.

ISBN: 81-7822-135-7